A TEXAS TRAGEDY:

The New London (TX) School Explosion

A Texas Tragedy:

The New London (TX) School Explosion

A Play in Two Acts

BOBBY H. JOHNSON

Stephen F. Austin State University Press
2012

For information, address Stephen F. Austin State University Press, 1936 North Street, LAN 203, Nacogdoches, Texas, 75962.

sfapress.sfasu.edu

Cover Image:
Charlotte Baker Montgomery
Night, Shacks and Flares, Kilgore
October, 1934
oil pastel
12 inches x 9 inches
92.001.24
Museum of East Texas Collection
Gift of the Artist

Cover design: Meagan Rice
Book design: Kristi Warren
Production assistants: Laura McKinney and Laura Davis

LIBRARY OF CONGRESS CATALOGING-IN-PUBLICATION DATA

Johnson, Bobby H.
A Texas Tragedy: The New London School Explosion / A Play in Two Acts / Bobby H. Johnson—1st ed.
p. cm.
ISBN-13: 978-1-936208-67-7

I. Title

First Edition: February 2012

ACKNOWLEDGMENTS

I would like to express my thanks to several individuals and entities who assisted me in preparing this treatment of the worst accident in American history involving school children:

- My family who told me about the New London disaster.
- The staff of the London Museum who provided valuable information.
- The Museum of East Texas and Director J.P. McDonald for allowing me to use Mrs. Montgomery's art work.
- Stephen F. Austin State University and the Department of History for encouraging me in all my scholarly activity, particularly Dr. Mark Barringer, Associate Dean of Liberal Arts, and Dr. Robert Mathis, former Chairman of the History Department.
- My interviewees for retelling the story.
- The staff of the Lamp-Lite Playhouse who facilitated the production of this play in 2005, particularly Director Sarah McMullan and the late Glenda White.
- My friend Jack Heifner, who taught me how to write a play.
- Dr. Fred Tarpley for his kind foreword.
- The staff of the Stephen F. Austin State University Press, especially Director Kimberly Verhines; Editors Laura McKinney and Kristi Warren; Design assistant Megan Rice
- The staff of the East Texas Research Center and Steen Library for providing sources.
- My wife, Myrna E. Johnson, who has served as my left hand in all my scholarly pursuits.

FOREWORD

Seventy-five years after the New London, Texas, school explosion instantaneously ended life for three hundred students, haunted memories of all who knew them, and hushed a community's discussion of an unspeakable event, the detailed story is now told. On March 18, 1937, Bobby H. Johnson was an infant in New London destined to become the scribe, oral historian, and dramatist for the tragedy.

His first-grade brother became a member of the exclusive circle of "survivors" by fluke: forgetting that his mother had given him permission to stay after school and play with a friend, he took an early bus home to safety. But his mind never erased the image of a cloud of dust in the direction of the school that he saw from his bus window a mile away. Dr. Johnson's parents found their rock-solid faith threatened by the questions raised on March 18, 1937, comforted somewhat by the preacher who comforted them with the wisdom of Tennyson's "There lives more faith in honest doubt . . . than in half the creeds" and in the scriptural promise that "Faith is the substance of things hoped for, the evidence of things not seen."

For the past forty years, Dr. Johnson has recorded numerous oral history interviews with New Londoners and East Texans and filed mental notes as he heard conversations about things that happened on that day when infancy protected his awareness of the horror in New London. I was in first grade in Leonard, Texas, 125 miles away, never conscious of the tragedy, probably because my parents wanted to shelter me. It was not until six years later when I was in elementary school in Hooks, Texas, that one of my teachers told my class the harrowing story of New London.

After her dramatic tale, we unnerved students cautiously walked the hallways sniffing the air for scents of odorized gas.

As an insider, Dr. Johnson was prepared for his role as the future New London dramatist by studies in history and journalism leading to a Ph.D. degree at the University of Oklahoma and the beginning of his career teaching history at Stephen F. Austin University, where he retired as a Regents Professor of History. He enrolled in a playwriting course taught at SFA by Jack Heifner, a Corsicana native and author of "Vanities," the most frequently performed American play of the 1970s. From the courses on crafting a play, Dr. Johnson mastered the final elements he needed to complete "A Texas Tragedy:" characterization, themes, and staging. From his appreciation of American literature, he understood how the stage manager in Thornton Wilder's "Our Town" orchestrated the themes and how poet Edgar Lee Masters handled ordinary people struggling with life in *Spoon River Anthology.* With a stage set of several acting areas anchored by a porch reminiscent of his parents' home, the acting area also accommodates a circle of truth platform where the preacher holds forth and witnesses enact a variety of personal encounters with the disaster. Hymn-singing groups set the tone for a grief-stricken community whose strong faith seeks resilience.

With flexibility in staging and foresight in allowing selection of scenes for productions by groups with different pools of acting talent and performing venues, Dr. Johnson's generosity permits school groups and little theater organizations to stage portions of "A Texas Tragedy" adapting the script as their resources permit. What a far cry from Eugene O'Neill, who would not allow a single word to be changed in the authorized script that he contracted for performances.

Healing after the explosion is said to have begun at the first reunion in 1977, forty years after the explosion. Audiences attending "A Texas Tragedy" will encounter a dignified, intensely moving tribute to the community robbed of a youthful generation, leaving scarred survivors overwhelmed by loss and questioning why it all happened. A forgetful public and those regarding New London as just another East Texas town will come away from "A Texas Tragedy" with factual details and emotional insights through the eyes of survivors into the nation's most devastating school disaster and its effect on people living in the world's most prosperous oil field.

By Fred Tarpley, Ph.D.

About Fred Tarpley

A fifth generation Northeast Texan, Fred Tarpley graduated from Hooks High School, received his first two degrees in journalism and English from East Texas State (now Texas A&M Commerce), and his Ph.D. in Linguistics from Louisiana State University. He taught college English for forty-four years, the last nine years at Jarvis Christian College, retiring as interim academic dean.

His research and writing focus on the language, literature, history, and folklore of Northeast Texas. His books include *Place Names of Northeast Texas, 1001 Texas Place Names, Southwest, Wood Eternal: The Story of Osage Orange, Bois d'Arc, etc.,* and a soon-to-be-completed study of 100,000 Texas geographic names.

He has served as president of the East Texas Historical Association, president of the American Names Society, director of the Place Name Survey of the United States, president of the Linguistics Association of the Southwest, executive director of the Texas Council of Teachers of English, and founding director of the Texas Interscholastic League Literature Criticism Contest. He currently advises the Silver Leos Writers Guild in Commerce and aids aspiring writers to progress toward publication.

Stories of the New London school explosion have been among his haunting memories since formative years.

CONTENTS

NEW LONDON MONUMENT - Dedicated in 1939, this monument or cenotaph stands on an island in front of the re-built school. Names of victims are inscribed on its base. (Photo courtesy of the author)

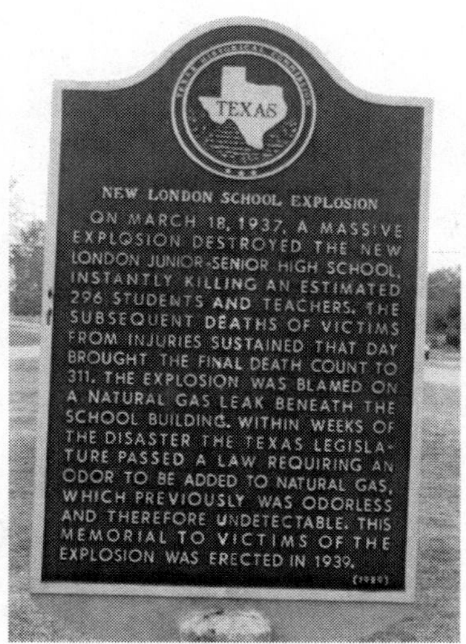

HISTORICAL MARKER - New London school explosion marker at entry to Pleasant Hill Cemetery. (Photo courtesy of the author)

INTRODUCTION

HISTORICAL BACKGROUND:

The New London School Explosion

Disasters have been the plague of humankind from time *in memoriam*. Wars, diseases, natural calamities, and a host of other factors have claimed untold millions throughout the ages, resulting in massive human suffering and despair. To a public accustomed to watching "breaking news" on television, disasters and violence are common fare. Explanations sometimes emerge but they often prove inconsequential in view of the element of chance in human existence (or Mother Nature?). Sometimes, there seems to be no answer as to why such things happen, especially when they involve children.

When their school blew up a few minutes before the final bell on March 18, 1937, the people of New London, Texas, quickly discerned the meaning of the word "disaster." The effects of this catastrophe on a rural area enmeshed in the social-economic changes brought on by the East Texas Oil Boom and the Great

---

* Portions of this essay are based on a presentation at the "Memory of Catastrophe" conference at Southampton University in England in 2000. About 100 scholars from Europe and the United States shared ideas on a variety of topics around the central theme of catastrophe. My co-author was Dr. J.B. Watson of the sociology department at Stephen F. Austin State University. I wish to thank Dr. Watson for his contributions on the sociological aspects of disaster.

Depression were overwhelming. About 300 persons died—mainly students in grades 5 through 11. Many others were injured. Today, nearly 75 years later, the pain inflicted on that community is still evident, although most of the parents and many of the survivors have since died. An imposing monument stands as a symbol of the worst school tragedy in the history of the United States. Across State Highway 42, a tasteful museum commemorates the event with displays featuring photographs, documents, and artifacts. All are fitting memorials to those who lost their lives, both literally and figuratively, on that fateful day. But the question remains: Why?

Despite these efforts to commemorate the horrific explosion, however, the facts are virtually unknown to most persons alive today, including many who live in East Texas. The absence of memory, both individual and collective, is not entirely due to the passage of time or a lack of interest in historical matters. The community itself attempted to escape the reality of what had happened. Some entire families moved away rather than live with daily reminders of the tragedy. Others were reluctant to talk about it for years. Indeed, a generation of parents went to their graves with the pent-up grief they had experienced. Finally, as parents and survivors began to die off and memories faded, the numbing effects of the explosion subsided, and survivors began to realize that recognition and acceptance likely would bring some relief. The community held its first reunion in 1977, the fortieth anniversary of the disaster, with others to follow. Memorial services and social events became a key part of the recovery process. A degree of closure had at last come to New London.

Over the years, I have accumulated numerous oral history interviews with both survivors and observers of the explosion and the area. Once simplified techniques of recording became available, oral history emerged as a useful tool for historians. It allows them to capture the memories of average persons which might otherwise go unrecorded. While the process of memory is subject to human failings, *i.e.*, with regard to accuracy and perspective, it is a means of capturing information on past events still within memory. The careful oral history practitioner must consider the pitfalls of bias and confusion, taking care to follow recommended procedures, particularly with regard to phrasing questions. Since 1970 I have conducted several hundred interviews on a variety of East Texas topics ranging from the Great Depression to the World War II home front. I have used this material to produce four memory plays on East Texas, including this play on New London.[1] These interviews, along with more traditional historical sources, particularly newspapers, have provided considerable perspective on the New London community and its inhabitants.

Located in the region known as East Texas (with a capital "E"), New London, and its predecessor Old London, about a mile away, were part of a community that dated back to the nineteenth century. This portion of the region is a rolling, gently-hilled area, with heavy forestation. It belies the popular image of Texas as a flat place covered by cactus. New London itself is located in the northwestern part of Rusk County, some 150 miles southeast of Dallas and about 190 miles north of Houston. The nearest town of any size in 1930 was Tyler, about 25 miles away. This part of East Texas remained a poor agricultural area until the discovery of oil. In fact, it struggled until the oil business brought a measure of prosperity to those fortunate enough to profit from the boom, especially land-holders who could sell oil rights to their property.

The establishment of New London reflected the growth of the oil field in Rusk County, named for an early Texas hero, Thomas Jefferson Rusk. It was not incorporated as a town until years later. Although East Texas is composed of numerous counties stretching from the Gulf coastal areas to the Oklahoma and Louisiana borders, the giant oil field was located mainly in Rusk and Gregg counties. The scope of this discovery likely transcended in value even the gold fields of California and Alaska. Nearly five billion barrels had been pumped from the East Texas field by the early 1990s. In addition to bringing Texas through the Depression, it fueled the great Allied war machine in World War II.

As the western-most extension of the Old South, early 20th century East Texas embodied the agrarian outlook associated with the post-Civil War era until the discovery of oil in 1930. Indeed, the oil boom made East Texas a magnet for job-seekers hard-hit by the Depression; As Clark and Halbouty note in *The*

Last Boom, it was the "greatest oil field ever seen on the North American continent."[2] More immediately, the oil boom resulted in dramatic population growth for East Texas. Small towns such as Henderson, Overton, and Kilgore and Longview doubled in size within a few months. City manager Bill N. Taylor noted that in Longview "suddenly you had to shove your way down the sidewalk." Job seekers who flooded into the area recall that they had to live in tents or even outdoors in the early days. Such growth also brought problems for local government.[3]

Not surprisingly, lawlessness plagued oil field communities during the early years of the boom. Petty crime such as gambling and prostitution was common, along with the more serious crimes of assault, robbery, and oil theft. Indeed, law enforcement officials often found themselves unable to handle such matters because of the rapid population growth and crowded conditions. Outside help often made the difference. For example, the famous Texas Ranger, M.T. "Lone Wolf" Gonzaulles, came to Kilgore early on in the boom and almost single-handedly deterred criminal activity. One young female attorney was especially impressed by Gonzaulles' impact upon the community. "He was called 'the law,'' she noted, and the cry of "here comes the law" would bring people running. "It was the first time I ever saw 'the law' walking," she added. At one point, the governor even ordered National Guard troops into the field to maintain order.

The oil boom also strained local schools, and district officials throughout the region often found it difficult to provide adequate facilities to accommodate the influx of children. In reality, the boom was a blessing in view of the potential increase in the tax rate, but in the short-run schools were filled to capacity. One teacher in Kilgore recalled that she had 75 children in one room. London schools faced a similar problem with as many as 85 students crammed into one room in 1931. Such desperate overcrowding led to the eventual construction of modern school plants at such places as Gaston, Leverett's Chapel, and, of course, New London, where the value of the physical plant was estimated at one million dollars in the mid-1930s. Money was the least problem in the world's largest oil field—a situation that later became ironic when the cause of the explosion came under investigation.

The development of a modern school system thus grew from meager beginnings in the London community. During the nineteenth century, small schools were often located within walking distance for most students. This was true in the London area, where such small places as Bunker Hill and Norfolk boasted primitive schools. One such school was built at Old London in 1872. This site continued to provide schooling for the London area until the coming of the oil field. In 1931 London became an independent school district with its own board of trustees and completed the construction of a new modern facility for the junior and senior high grades at New London. It was this building that was destined for the disastrous events of March 18, 1937. The elementary school for grades one through four was located several hundred yards away. The district also owned a fleet of buses marked in the school colors of blue and gold. The community took considerable pride in such modern facilities--it even had a lighted football field—lacking in most area schools.

My family became associated with the schools when my brother, Joe Mack, entered the first grade in the fall of 1936. My mother and father, Johnye McLemore Johnson and Harold R. Johnson, had grown up in southeastern Oklahoma near McAlester. Both came from farm backgrounds; they married in 1929, just in time to experience the Great Depression that followed the financial crash of that year. In 1933 they came to East Texas where my father found work in a Kilgore store until he went to work for the Humble Oil & Refining Company. They soon moved to New London, where my father built a small "shotgun" house not far from the school. His employment was a godsend in view of the economic conditions because jobs were hard to find, and employment with a major company like Humble brought a degree of security. He first worked as a common laborer building pipe racks and digging ditches. He later became a meter man who checked charts on oil- and gas-producing facilities. In fact, he was doing just that on a lease not far from the school when he heard the explosion. Along with several hundred relief workers, most of them oil field employees, he helped in the recovery process, struggling to clear wreckage and uncover bodies. It was a haunting experience.

Less than two miles away on that fated March day in 1937, a young housewife (my mother) awaited the arrival of one of those buses. It was past 3 p.m. and the bus should appear any minute. She had apparently forgotten that she had told her first-grader that he could stay at school and play with a neighborhood friend whose mother was attending a PTA meeting. (He in turn forgot and boarded the early bus.) She and a neighbor lady were visiting in the back yard when they heard a loud noise, which the neighbor attributed to a boiler explosion in the oil field—a fairly common occurrence—but they quickly noticed a cloud of dust in the direction of the school. Much to her relief, her son soon stepped off the bus a short distance away from the little house where her other son lay sleeping. Years later, that first-grader (my brother) recalled watching the building explode from a bus window a mile or so away. He had been in the auditorium practicing for a program scarcely an hour before the explosion.[4] Earlier that day, the meeting had been moved from the school auditorium to the gymnasium a few yards behind the fated building—a fortunate move as it turned out. The auditorium was destroyed but the gymnasium a few yards away remained intact.

Something had gone terribly wrong, and the outcome would be catastrophic. School Superintendent W.C. Shaw, who was just outside the building, later told the Associated Press that he did not hear much noise, although one rescue worker said his father heard the blast in Cushing, twenty-five miles away. Tenth grader Horace Grigg later recalled that he had no particular memory of any sound, but Martha Leath Moore, who was in the sewing lab, remembered a loud noise before "everything went black." About a mile away, Henry Pittman heard a boom which he also assumed to be an exploding boiler before he looked out an office window and saw the building disintegrating.

Once word of the explosion began to spread the noise reverberated around the world. A few telephone calls to surrounding towns brought quick responses from rescue workers and the media. Because the explosion occurred shortly before the end of the school day, it would not be reported by most newspapers until the following day, except for a few "extra" editions. Area radio stations, however, aired the story almost immediately. What followed was a torrent of reportage, including facts, rumors, and misinformation, particularly the body count. Early headlines placed the death toll at anywhere from 300 to 700 persons. *The New York Times*, for example, ran the following banner headline above its front-page account of March 19: "500 Pupils Are Killed in Explosion of Texas School." The *Dallas Morning News* proclaimed "700 Children Thought Dead as Blast Razes Rusk County School Building." The Tyler *Courier-Times'* extra edition on the same date reported between 300 and 400 killed, citing a statement from Supt. Shaw. Some thirty-five miles from New London, the Tyler paper dispatched staff members to the site within an hour of the explosion, as did the Henderson *Daily News*. *The New York Times* had a man on the scene that night after the arrival of veteran reporter Meyer Berger, who had been in Houston covering another story. Berger hired a taxi to take him the 190 miles to New London.[5]

Working under adverse conditions, the news media did a commendable job in reporting the story. Limited telephone communication was frustrating, leading many correspondents to rely on the Western Union office in Overton. Considerable misinformation occurred early on, particularly with regard to the number of fatalities. A lot of speculation also involved the cause of the explosion, ranging from gas seepage from the earth to leaks in the heating system. Perhaps the most colorful comment came from one local paper when it solemnly declared in a sub-headline: "Probably More Children Killed Thursday in Blast than any Other Catastrophe since Biblical Flood." The discovery of several sticks of dynamite in a remote storage area even led to theories that the building was purposefully blown up, but authorities quickly squelched the rumor.

The basic facts were known: an explosion had occurred, numerous persons had died, and the community was in a state of shock. With hundreds of rescue workers, parents, and onlookers clogging the area, it was difficult to make sense of the event. Some order appeared as law enforcement personnel arrived on the scene and work crews became organized. Moreover, Texas governor James V. Allred's quick decision to impose martial law encouraged civil order and implemented an early investigation. Once it began in a day or so, news sources had more facts to report.

For those who observed the explosion site, the former school suddenly became a tangle of tile bricks, roofing, timbers, steel girders, and mortar dust. Several chunks of debris, weighing as much as a ton, were hurled more than fifty yards away by the blast, some landing on automobiles parked in front of the school. One eyewitness, Raymond Bonner, said the building "went up like a dynamited stump." Principal F.F. Waggoner said he had just left the building, thereby missing death or injury by about ten yards. He was quoted in a news account as saying that "he never wanted to enter another school building." (But he did, later leaving New London for school work elsewhere.) An elementary school teacher, Christene Beasley, was in the school cafeteria, fifty or so yards from the fated building when it exploded. She ran outside after hearing the boom but had to dodge falling debris. (She later taught me in the third grade.) As she approached the rubble she stumbled over children's bodies. Mrs. Tom Parmley, a playground supervisor who was about twenty yards from the site, said she had to seek shelter in a parked car to avoid flying debris. She had to step out of the way to avoid being hit by another student who jumped from a window. She reported that one young girl later died in her hands.

Mildred Jones Evans, a second-grade teacher, was attending the PTA meeting in the gymnasium. When the explosion occurred, she looked out of the windows and noticed large trees swaying before a thick cloud of dust enveloped the scene. She first thought of her young son in her house less than a hundred yards away. She reported that the dust became so thick that it hindered her view. Somehow she assisted in getting the elementary children, who had been performing a folk dance at the meeting, back to their building before checking on her home. Her husband Carroll Evans was a high school science teacher who had left work early to pack for a trip. He asked a friend, Willie Tate, to cover his class during the last period. Tate died in the explosion. The science room was destroyed.[6]

The precise number of students in the school at the time of the explosion is unknown, but it is likely that it numbered more than six hundred.[7] The sheer terror of the explosion left most survivors numbed and confused, but the passage of time allowed many survivors and observers to recall the scene quite vividly, as the following comments from oral history interviews reveal.

Max Holleyman, an eleventh grader, was attending Mr. Garner's history class when the explosion occurred. He said that he first sought refuge under a desk in the dust-filled room before jumping out of a window. Not seriously injured, he began to look for his sister, a sixth grader, but had no success. He later drove a teacher's car to a business near the Humble Company office and telephoned for help. Unfortunately, his sister died in the disaster.

Horace Grigg, a seventeen-year-old student, did not hear the explosion from his seat in a plane geometry class in the north wing of the building. In fact, he did not know what had happened until he awoke the following Tuesday in a Kilgore hospital.[8] He suffered a concussion and a broken back, remaining in the hospital for a month. His brother, Edwin, a seventh-grader, died in the explosion.

Another student in the same math class, Arthur Shaw, a nephew of Supt. Shaw, had vivid memories of the experience. Shaw reported that the class was "misbehaving" because the teacher was out of the room. He recalled that he was buried under fallen plaster and wire, his eyes filled with mortar dust. Two friends extracted him from the wreckage, he said, and took him to the cafeteria before he was driven to the Baptist church in Overton where a dentist and a beauty operator sewed up a wound on his head. He spent several days in the new Mother Frances Hospital in Tyler, which opened a day early to treat New London victims. His own grief was heightened by the fact that his sister and a cousin, Sambo Shaw, son of the superintendent, died in the explosion.

Another student, Myrtle Moore, an eleventh-grader, escaped serious injury in the high school study hall where she was awaiting the final bell, shortly after 3 p.m. She had just stood up, she said, when the building exploded. Her first memory was of a large slab of rubble that fell across her desk. A school mate urged her to follow him out a second story window, but she froze on the window sill—the sight of bodies outside frightened her. She finally managed to crawl through the debris and escape down a stairwell. With books and pencils in hand, she observed several bodies laid out on a rise near the school. In the background, she heard a chorus of wailing onlookers. She was taken to Overton in a laundry truck but soon returned because she knew that her father, Jack Moore, a custodian in the elementary school, would be worried. She later learned that he had left the building only moments before the blast, thereby escaping injury. He had been there to collect mail for the elementary school.

Another student, Martha Leath, recounted a similar experience. She had been working on her senior prom dress in the sewing room not far from the study hall. About twenty girls were present in the room, which took considerable damage. She had no memory of how she escaped from the building but found herself standing on the nearby football field, dazed and covered with mortar dust yet unhurt except for scratches. She carried her prom dress folded over her arm. (She later wore it to a make-shift prom.) Although she wanted to remain at the site, her father insisted that they go home because her mother would be worried. When her aunts arrived from Henderson the next morning, they brought red flowers because they feared that their niece was dead.

A diverse crowd quickly gathered at the blast site, including anxious family members seeking loved ones and oil field workers who came to clear the wreckage and rescue the wounded. They were sometimes one and the same. The oil companies dispatched large gangs of workers to the site along with the necessary equipment for rescue. These workers, young and old, were the unsung heroes of the disaster; their labors throughout the night and well into the next day unearthed numerous survivors as well as hundreds of bodies. Theirs' was a gruesome task that haunted many of them for the rest of their lives.

Henry Pittman, who saw the building blow up, estimated that he arrived within a few minutes of the explosion. As one of the first to arrive on the scene, he aided in the early rescue of several children stranded in the wreckage. He worked until dark, helping to clear the rubble that stood eight to ten feet high; he returned early the next day to continue the task. Pittman said some of the bodies were terribly mangled. "I saw men work and cry at the same time," he said. He completed his efforts by digging graves at Pleasant Hill Cemetery, where more than a hundred of the victims are buried.

Harold R. Johnson also had a close-up view of the catastrophe. He was among the Humble Company employees sent to the disaster site. He worked all night, stopping only for rest breaks and coffee provided by the Red Cross and Salvation Army. Over the next few days he assisted family members who flooded into the area seeking to comfort their bereaved relatives. An Oklahoma farm boy who had migrated to East Texas in the boom, Johnson was ill-prepared for what he saw. The ordeal contributed to a variety of physical and nervous ailments that plagued him for years—an early case of shell shock or Post Traumatic Stress Disorder as it has become known. "He couldn't get it off his mind," his wife said. For several years he suffered nausea virtually every morning after breakfast, she added.

Others also rushed to the scene, among them oil field worker Clint Howard. He was returning from a trip to Tyler when he heard the news over his car radio. Avoiding the already crowded highways by traveling back roads, he hurried to the school and joined the horde of workers already there. He, too, worked through the night, often joining a line to "hand off bricks" and other bits of rubble—a sort of "basket brigade" like those used in the 9/11 disaster in New York City. "It was pitiful," Howard said, "the worst thing you could ever think of."

The experience was particularly impressionable on young rescuers. Barnie Bigby was working on a rig-building crew not far away when he heard about the mishap. He spent several hours on the clean-up. Only seventeen years old, Bigby was deeply moved by the sight of bodies. Another youngster, Jack Gray of Henderson, was working at Henderson High School when word of the explosion arrived. "We were lining the field for the county meet set for the next day," he said. Athletes from New London and other county schools were scheduled to participate in the track meet. Gray and several high school friends immediately headed for New London in a Model A Ford. They, too, spent several hours working at the site. Years later, both Bigbie and Gray would experience the blood-shed of battle in World War II, Bigbie in the first wave of the invasion at Iwo Jima, and Gray at Normandy. Sadly, New London had prepared them for death and destruction.

Others experienced trauma at various stages of the tragedy, including Lucille Fain, a young reporter for the Nacogdoches *Daily Sentinel*. She visited the Crim Funeral Home in Henderson soon after the explosion. Even though she had viewed bodies earlier in her career, she winced at the sight of children on large mortuary slabs. Her story the next day confirmed how painful it was to view "lifeless little bodies in patched overalls and blood-stained gingham dresses." J.N. Beard had a similar experience when he served as a pallbearer at several funerals. An employee of the Humble Company, he was recuperating from a recent oil field injury when his boss sent him from Gladewater in Gregg County to assist in any way possible. He recalled that funeral directors were so over-burdened that numerous volunteers assisted in loading and unloading caskets from pick-up trucks often used in place of proper funeral vehicles. Beard, too, found his experience traumatic. Nina Murphy, a high school student from Henderson, recalled that she went to the blast scene to search for her cousin, Blondell Maxwell, a ninth-grader who lived with their grandparents. While her grandmother remained in the car, Nina took a scrap of cloth from the dead girl's dress and showed it to her grandmother, who recognized it.

As the shocked community began the task of burying its children, the sheer magnitude of the disaster became obvious. Some seventy-five embalmers worked night and day identifying and preparing the bodies, which had been taken to several funeral homes throughout the area. Many churches cancelled their regular Sunday services so the facilities would be available for funerals. Weary area ministers, many of whom had rested little since the explosion, conducted several services a day, as grief-stricken families faced yet another trial burying their children. Make-shift choral groups moved from grave to grave singing such Gospel songs as "Asleep in Jesus" and "No Tears in Heaven." Perhaps the saddest commentary appeared in the Henderson paper, which noted in its Sunday edition that five "paper carriers" from its circulation department had been victims of the explosion. "They won't bring your newspaper this morning," the article explained.

Some of the most vivid accounts were written by Meyer Berger of *The New York Times,* who had covered the story virtually from its beginning. His description of a mother "borne up by her tight-jawed husband" is illustrative of his stories. "So it went all day," he continued. "In London, Shiloh, Kilgore, Longview, Tyler—in communities covering an area of some forty square miles, the scene was multiplied over and over, until the blue sky darkened with sunset." He described the funeral processions as "the most pitiful cavalcade this nation has ever known." [9]

A military Court of Inquiry initiated a prompt investigation, in keeping with Governor Allred's call for an immediate inquiry. Proper legislative action soon followed, thereby allowing the state to hold an inquiry under martial law. Proceedings began on Saturday, March 20, less than two days after the explosion. Representatives of committees from the Texas Legislature and the U.S. Bureau of Mines attended and later issued their own reports. Maj. Gaston Howard presided over the hearing, assisted by two colonels and three captains, all from the Texas National Guard. More than thirty witnesses testified, including Superintendent Shaw, representatives of the architectural firm that had designed the building, and other pertinent individuals who shared technical knowledge. Dr. E.P. Schoch, a professor of chemistry from the University of Texas, played an important role in the investigation, along with other experts. The court met in the school band hall, located in a separate building. Numerous press representatives thus reported on the unfolding revelations while the community planned funerals.[10]

The investigations explored numerous theories on why the accident happened, ranging from stray gas to questionable plumbing procedures. Few persons could have predicted such a disaster, especially in an oil field community where most people understood the deadly potential of natural gas—certainly not those who heated their own homes and churches with the odorless substance taken from the interior of the earth. Because the school administration had approved a change in the gas supply several weeks earlier, much of the focus revolved around that transaction. In an effort to save about $250 a month, board members had switched from commercial service and tapped into a waste gas line from a nearby plant.[11] Much of the community, including several churches and many homes, was already using the free waste gas.

As the building architect revealed, the original plans had called for steam heating supported by a remote boiler, but the school authorities had instead chosen a system that used some seventy-two individual gas-steam heaters. This necessitated numerous gas lines under the foundation. The report ultimately concluded that a leaking gas line likely caused the explosion, probably ignited by a spark in the manual arts room that had access to the area under the building. Because the site was destroyed by the explosion and tons of wreckage prevailed, more specific information would never be known.[12] In view of such uncertainty, some members of the community blamed the administration for causing the disaster, and a number of lawsuits followed. Ultimately, a civil court held that no blame should be assigned. President Franklin D. Roosevelt called upon the Red Cross for assistance, and the state government quickly enacted a law requiring the addition of an odorant to natural gas, in addition to stronger regulatory laws on school facilities.

School officials quickly determined that school should resume as soon as possible, Less than two weeks after the explosion, classes began in temporary quarters elsewhere on campus. Attendance was down at first, but students eventually returned to finish a shortened term, deemed important to graduating students and the community, despite the numbing effects of such a disaster. Community members and school officials also determined that a new school should replace the destroyed campus. As noted earlier, these developments took on sociological meaning as the community groped for answers. Unlike modern disaster scenes, New London could not rely on governmental agencies such as today's Federal Emergency Management Agency (FEMA) and other relief programs.

As noted earlier the community became traumatized. This is in keeping with the later investigations of Yale sociologist Kai Erikson, whose book, *A New Species of Trouble: Explorations in Disaster, Trauma, and Community,* argues for a broader definition of trauma to take in the entire community.[13] New London was truly a traumatized community in need of healing. That process began with the construction of a memorial monument in 1939. It was a sign of progress, even though some parents did not want their childrens' names placed on it. The large cenotaph was funded by contributions from school children across the state as well as other individuals, groups, and corporations. Designed by Texas artist Herring Coe, the granite memorial depicts twelve life-sized figures of school children and teachers. Later, in 1977, the community held a reunion (now held biennially), but it had taken forty years of pain before such healing became accepted.

During the period between the explosion and that first reunion, a code of silence prevailed as many persons were reluctant to discuss the disaster. (I faced this problem when I first tried to gather information in 1970.) Later interviews revealed that supportive services commonly provided in modern catastrophes were largely absent at New London. Apparently little professional counseling was available; consequently, churches, friends, and family members provided whatever social support survivors received. Reluctance to talk about the event, as revealed by several of our interviewees, perhaps delayed effective coping and long-term healing. As Myrtle Moore Carpenter commented, "I wanted to forget it—I had lost too many friends." She said that news reports of the Oklahoma City disaster later reopened wounds. "I knew what they were going through." Martha Leath Moore said it was twenty-five years before she could talk about the disaster. "You just lived with it and did the best you could. . . It got the best of some people," she added.[14]

As New London approaches the upcoming (2012) seventy-fifth anniversary of the tragedy, the number of survivors has dwindled, just as the community has changed. Now known as West Rusk, the result of several consolidations over the years, the high school continues to use the rebuilt building, which, despite its age, remains a handsome edifice. The decline of the oil field after World War II led to a population loss for the area, although East Texas has shown considerable growth. New London has been incorporated into a small city of about a thousand persons, and its residents take pride in the presence of the Museum, which draws many visitors. Surprisingly, not much has been written about the disaster, except for a few books and a couple of television documentaries. This will likely change as the seventy-fifth anniversary approaches. Newspapers continue to show interest in the subject, usually in conjunction with the biyearly reunions. For a community that tried to forget its past, New London nevertheless continues to hold an important historical presence. It remains the site of the worst disaster involving school children in United States history.

MAKING A PLAY

How I Wrote *A Texas Tragedy*

As a young boy I grew up in the shadow of the explosion. My family lived in New London until 1947, and I attended school there through the fifth grade. I returned to teach in East Texas in 1966 after completing graduate study in both journalism and history. I have spent about two-thirds of my life in this area; therefore, I have come to know the region and the people I write about. Such a background further prepared me for writing the New London story, along with my specialized use of oral history. As I reflect upon these things, I believe it was a story meant for me. I had to write about it.

"A Texas Tragedy" has been nearly twenty years in the making. I began work on this project in the 1990s, when I became actively involved with the Lamp-Lite Playhouse in Nacogdoches. In 1991 I wrote a New London scene into my first memory play, "East Texas Remembers," with the aid of my collaborators Sarah McMullan and the late Glenda White.[15] Later, I decided to write a play on the mishap rather than a book, which would have been more in keeping with my profession as an historian. The main problem was that I was not familiar with the process of writing a play. Being on a university campus, I decided to take a course on playwriting. Fortunately, my university had a seasoned playwright conducting just such a course. Jack Heifner, a native Texan, is best known for his off-Broadway play, "Vanities" (now in a musical version). He taught me how to tell a story with proper stage technique—I learned about the need for conflict and resolution, as well as a message delivered by properly developed characters. I took his advice and produced a play. I owe him a great deal: the result is what you will be reading.

I chose to tell the story through the eyes of my parents, a young couple who lived in New London when the disaster unfolded. As noted earlier, my father was a country boy who came to the oil field looking for work; he had mouths to feed. My mother was a diligent housewife who wanted to make her family happy. They tried, only to be dealt a blow by fate: a terrible, tragic thing that threatened their happiness. How they handled the New London tragedy is at the heart of the story. My parents' experiences, while heavily dramatized, reflected those of perhaps thousands of others who had to deal with New London. Death, or even the threat of death, haunts the minds of those who see their children in danger. For that reason I chose to speak through a preacher and his religion—a perfectly natural thing considering the East Texas community of that day. This decision also lent itself to my resolution that involved an epiphany or sudden revelation that defies easy explanation—the kind of thing that happens to Harry Jones at the end of this play.

I began by gathering information from a variety of sources. Newspaper accounts, oral history interviews, and government records provided me with sufficient material to tell the story, but, as I learned, it was a complicated event, riddled with rumors, speculation and human pathos. Using the genre of drama, I learned, was both intellectually exciting and a bit problematic. I wanted it be historically correct, but I realized that I would have to supplement the historical record with fictional characters and dialogue. Otherwise, I would have a mass of information but no story.

Seeking a model, I turned to Thornton Wilder's "Our Town," a play about a New England town in the early twentieth century. I had earlier seen and read the play, and I found it fascinating; the New London experience presented a haunting sense of *dejavu*. In re-reading it (and, later playing the role of Howie the milkman in a local production of the play) I had the same haunting feelings about life and death. Wilder's use of a stage manager (or narrator) provided a pattern for my "Preacher" character. I was also influenced by the poet Edgar Lee Master's "Spoon River Anthology," a series of poems about ordinary people and their struggles with life told from their graves. My use of a "witness" chair allowed some of my characters to speak directly to the audience. These are often verbatim from my interviews with slight literary flourishes. (I made up a few, but I trust they are in keeping with the truth.)[16]

Before writing this play, I prepared a detailed outline in which I tried to "see" each scene as it unfolded. The actual writing began in March of 2003, and it went fairly quickly. I did considerable re-writing during the process, which later included a public reading that allowed me to query viewers about their reactions to the play. Further re-writing followed. I usually work at night (in a little cabin in my back yard), and I often watch television as I write (perhaps my journalistic background allows me to do two things at the same time.) While I view my task as a satisfying experience, it was somewhat depressing as I recalled my parents' role in the disaster. (They both are deceased.) My brother's close call also haunted me.

The result of my efforts is a two-act play of about two hours with a brief intermission. It was performed in the spring of 2005 as part of the Lamp-Lite's 2004-2005 series. Capacity crowds (about 215 seats) viewed the six performances. A wide array of persons saw the play, including several survivors. The cast included about twenty-five actors, although some doubling of parts may reduce that figure. A simple stage setting is anchored by a back porch with steps and swinging screen door upstage, and two platforms downstage left and right. One platform will be a "circle of light" with a plain podium; the other will be the witness chair, with perhaps a small table holding a tape recorder. Other scenes will unfold in the middle area—the destruction scene, a school house scene, etc.—but the porch will be central because that is where the young couple do much of their talking. Lighting should be varied, with shades of red and blue depicting tense dramatic action. Properties will be minimal. At the end of the play, a screen emerges for the showing of appropriate scenes—the school buildings, the monument, the destruction, and a few individuals. This should be accompanied by a piano softly playing the school song, "London Oh London".[17]

The characters in this play are a sampling of the community, ranging from students and teachers to oilfield workers and journalists. If there has to be a "lead" character it is "Preacher," because he appears more often. Bonnie and Harry Jones, the young couple, also merit attention because it is their story. To me, the "witnesses" play a key role in view of their varied but pertinent comments based on their poignant perspectives. Whatever they portray, the characters are all important because they contribute to the span of personalities involved in this horrible incident.

As I reflect upon the significance of my contribution, I admit that it is not Shakespeare—nor Wilder or Miller, but it is a story that has largely been forgotten. In publishing this play, I hope not only to reach a larger audience but also to make it available for public school use, whether for one-act plays or readings.[18] Community theatres are also encouraged to consider it for presentation. Users are free to make necessary cuts or adaptations with permission of the author. Interested persons may gain further information by contacting the Stephen F. Austin State University Press.

ENDNOTES

[1] Copies of these scripts, along with many of my tapes and transcripts, are available in the East Texas Research Center of Steen Library on the Stephen F. Austin State University campus in Nacogdoches. The plays dealt with the first half of the twentieth-century, including such topics as the Great Depression, the East Texas Oil Boom, the history of SFA, and the home front in World War II.

[2] For an account of the East Texas Oil Boom, see James A. Clark and Michael T. Halbouty, *The Last Boom* (New York, 1972).

[3] For a fuller treatment of social conditions, see Bobby H. Johnson, "Oil in the Pea Patch: The East Texas Oil Boom," *East Texas Historical Journal*, Vol. XIII (Spring, 1975), pp. 34-41. A version of this paper was delivered at the Western Historical Association meeting in New Haven, Conn., in 1972.

[4] Many years later, my mother vividly recounted the events of that day. Much of the following information was obtained in oral

history interviews in the author's possession.

[5] Later in his career, Berger received a Pulitzer Prize for his reporting on crime in New York. Two other journalists destined for later fame also covered the disaster: Sarah McClendon for the Tyler paper and Walter Cronkite for the United Press.

[6] Mrs. Evans told me that her husband experienced a considerable amount of guilt over his dead colleague for the rest of his life. Interview with Mildred Jones Evans, Henderson, TX., July 17, 1997.

[7] Mollie Sealey Ward, the founding director of the London Museum, estimated that about 650 students were in the building, based on her study of the disaster.

[8] Interview with Horace Grigg, Carlsbad, N.M., July 24, 1997. His experience is recounted in a tense hospital scene in the play, along with a dramatic fictional scene at the end of the play.

[9] *The New York Times*, March 21, 1937.

[10] Perhaps the best treatment of this part of the tragedy is Michael L. Toon, "The New London Explosion," an M.A. thesis produced at Stephen F. Austin State University in 1977. Dr. Archie P. McDonald chaired this study and I served on the committee. Other pertinent information is available in Lori Olson, *New London School: In Memoriam. March 18, 1937, 3:17 P.M.* (Austin: Eakin Press, 2001.)

[11] Considered waste gas, this petro-chemical substance was piped back into the ground or flared off. It was also known as "green gas."

[12] Copies of these reports are available at the New London Museum archives.

[13] This work was published in 1994 by W. W. Norton.

[14] Reaction to later disasters often triggers memories. Doubtless many New London survivors were reminded of their experiences after the 9/11 crisis.

[15] My use of oral history in plays, while somewhat novel to me in 1990, proved to be fortunate. Thanks to these two women, I learned that re-telling such stories on the stage can be effective. The result was my "East Texas Remembers" series. A leading oral history scholar, Paul Thompson, suggested the staging of interviews in his book, *The Voices of the Past* (Oxford University Press, 1978).

[16] A good example of the effectiveness of monologues is Brian Friel's play "Molly Sweeny." He uses three actors who speak directly to the audience. It concerns a blind Irish woman's struggle to acquire sight after many years of blindness, only to learn that she was happier blind. The idea of witnesses is from "Reds," a 1981 movie by Warren Beatty concerning the journalist John Reed's involvement in the Russian Revolution early in the twentieth century.

[17] Words of the school song are as follows:

"London Oh London your colors of blue
Always remind us of loyalty true.
Deep in our hearts are your standards of gold.
May we ever laud you while ages roll.

[18] A one-act version of "A Texas Tragedy" was staged in district competition by Huntington (TX) High School in 2008, under the direction of Mrs. Amber Wagnon.

ABOUT THE AUTHOR

Bobby H. Johnson is a retired Regents Professor of History at Stephen F. Austin State University. He is the co-author of *Wiley Post, His Winnie Mae, and the World's First Pressure Suit* (Washington: Smithsonian Institution and Government Printing Office, 1971). He also wrote *The Coushatta People* (Phoenix: Indian Tribal Series, 1977). Additionally, he compiled and edited a series of interviews, *From Pine Trees to Paper: Interviews with Southland Paper Employees* (Center for East Texas Studies, Stephen F. Austin State University, 2002). The author of numerous scholarly papers, he has spoken before many scholarly groups, including The Western History Association, the Oral History Association, and the Texas State Historical Association. In 2008 he received the Life-time Achievement Award from the Texas Oral History Association for his collection of several hundred interviews, primarily on East Texas. These resulted in four "memory" plays, all under the general title of "East Texas Remembers," presented at the Lamp-Lite from 1991 through 2009. He holds an M.A. (University of Oklahoma School of Journalism, 1962) and a Ph.D. in history from the University of Oklahoma (1967). He taught history at Stephen F. Austin State University from 1966 to 2005. He is married to Myrna E. Johnson Johnson and they live in Nacogdoches, TX. They have two daughters—Melanie White of Burleson, TX, and Lara King, who lives in England; both are teachers.

SHOTGUN HOUSE - Oilfield house portrayed by artist Charlotte Baker Montgomery. Note the porch. (Used by permission of Museum of East Texas in Lufkin, where Mrs. Montgomery's works are based.)

ORIGINAL SCHOOL - The junior-senior high school building that blew up in 1937. Serving students in grades 5-11, it dated from the early 1930's. (Photo courtesy of New London Museum)

DISASTER SCENE - A view of part of the building after the explosion. Note the bread delivery van used to transport victims to first aid sites and hospitals. (Photo courtesy of New London Museum)

RECOVERY - Victims being removed from wreckage. Volunteers worked throughout the night to rescue victims and recover bodies. (Photo courtesy of New London Museum)

BODY REMOVAL - The Texas National Guard assisted in the recovery of bodies from the explosion site.
(Photo courtesy of New London Museum)

INTERSTATE EDITION
Price 5 Cents

THE HOUSTON CHRONICLE

670 FEARED DEAD IN SCHOOL BLAST; 300 BODIES RECOVERED

Mothers Fight Over Mangled Bodies of Children

Martial Law Ordered For E. Texas Tow

Bodies of Victims Badly Mangled; Pupils, Teachers Trapped As Explosion Rips Building to Bits.

By Associated Press

TWO MILLION STRIKERS TIE PARIS WORK

Partial List Of Dead And Injured

"Help Them Over There-- Come Back for Me Later," Buried Young Hero Cries

"I've Been To Hell," Says Newswriter

GRUESOME NEWS - Front page of the *Houston Chronicle,* March 19, 1937. A story repeated in newspapers throughout the nation.
(Photo courtesy of New London Museum)

TOMBSTONE - More than a hundred victims are buried in Pleasant Hill Cemetery. Note the photograph and inscription.
(Photo courtesy of the author)

TEACHER-STUDENT GUIDE

About the Play. . .

This guide is presented in conjunction with the publication of "A Texas Tragedy: The New London School Explosion," a two-act play about the worst school disaster in U.S. history. First presented at the Lamp-Lite Playhouse in early 2005, the play was part of a series about East Texas under the general title of "East Texas Remembers." It utilized oral history interviews, newspapers, and other historical sources. Some fictionalization was necessary to make a story, but it is based on a real event that happened in 1937. The play is aimed at a general audience as well as teachers and students who might want to use it both in the class-room and for dramatic contests. The following suggestions might be useful in an educational setting.

In a general sense, this play offers readers the opportunity to explore the significance of disaster in human events. Countless examples may be called up from history, including wars and political turmoil; natural events (such as droughts, storms, floods, etc.); disease and epidemics; and numerous other events or circumstances that have plagued humankind through the ages. The play is suitable for students as young as fifth-graders up through middle school and high school. (The actual disaster involved students in just such grades.)

It should be noted that "A Texas Tragedy" is not a documentary, although it has some of the qualities of such a genre. Rather, it is a drama largely based on first-hand accounts and contemporary news reporting. It is reminiscent of the works of Ken Burns, who brilliantly showed the effectiveness of combining words, pictures, and music in his treatment of the Civil War. My characters offer readers (or audiences) the chance to experience tragedy with all its darkness.

For Teachers. . .

Teachers may find it useful as a springboard into a number of topics associated with disaster. Foremost among these is the effect of tragedy on human beings (and, by extension, the community); the following questions are pertinent:

(1) How do individuals perceive disaster?
(2) What are their reactions to such events?
(3) What role should the government play (at all levels) in dealing with such disruption?
(4) On a personal level, is religion a suitable tool in dealing with such catastrophes?
(5) What about the role of counseling?

More specifically teachers may choose to focus on the era—in this case, the 1930s. What else was happening in this time frame? What was the effect of the Great Depression and Franklin Roosevelt's New Deal on peoples' perceptions? What was Roosevelt's role in the New London disaster? How did the rise of turmoil in Europe, *viz*, Hitler's rise in Germany and the resultant world war a few years later affect this era? Was the explosion a foreboding of worse days ahead? (Mention Adolf Hitler's telegram—get a copy from Museum.) Although modern students may think of the 1930s as ancient history, it was a memorable era that foretold modern times. Indeed, the event that thrust New London into the spotlight was widely reported both nationally and abroad by newspapers, radio stations, and news reels. (See introduction.) And yet, it is ancient history to most people alive today. Few persons below 50 years of age know about the disaster, even in East Texas where it occurred.

In addition, use of this play may lead to a unit on personal losses—deaths, wars and disasters. Perhaps teachers will wish to devote a unit in history and social science to the study of communities, especially how they are affected by disasters (often man-made) and freaks of nature (tornadoes and hurricanes). Some attention should be devoted to modern events and the way they are handled by governmental and quasi-governmental agencies. In recent times, the Federal Emergency Management Agency (FEMA) has played an increasingly important role in the treatment of communities beset by disaster. In earlier times, the Red Cross and Salvation Army provided auxiliary aid, as was the case in the New London explosion. President Roosevelt's first action was to call upon the services of the Red Cross, which resulted in much of the early relief. A Salvation Army team served on-site coffee and snacks on the night of the disaster, a service warmly received by relief workers and anguished parents. Special attention should be given to the relief workers, mainly oilfield hands and neighbors who spent the entire night clearing the site and recovering bodies. Many later worked as grave-diggers and also assisted at funerals. Area clergy and funeral home personnel also aided the community by planning funerals and providing counseling to anguished families.

For Students. . . .

Thus far the emphasis has been on teachers, but students should also participate through projects and research suited to their age groups. For instance, they might focus on the concept of commemoration, an important factor in any disaster. Modern examples are evident in storm-stricken communities and terroristic sites. At New London the public provided a memorial monument, a handsome obelisk which includes in its base the names of most of those killed in the disaster. Located in an esplanade in front of the re-built school, the granite marker is topped by a sculpture of several students and a teacher. It was dedicated in 1939. In our case, a day-trip to New London would allow students to visit the explosion site. In addition, students should tour the London Museum just across the highway. By visiting these sites, students may experience the deep reverence of the community. Teachers may arrange visits by calling the Museum (phone: (903) 895-4602) New London is located in Rusk County about ten miles northwest of Henderson. (School groups are encouraged.)

Before visiting the site, students may be prepared by various projects involving research in old newspapers and other printed materials, with particular attention to other disasters in Texas City (1947) and Galveston (1900). Some may choose to focus on the great disaster in Nova Scotia where a ship exploded in 1917, killing about 1,800 persons. Additionally, they may participate in class-room scenarios drawn from the play.

High school students and their advisers are encouraged to perform cuttings of the play in competition sponsored by the Interscholastic League. (Note: Texas schools may use my play free of any royalty payment.) A time limit of forty minutes will challenge directors to choose those elements best-suited to their judgment and resources. Please feel free to consult with me if you wish. I may be reached at this website: bobbyjohnsonphd@yahoo.com. My wish is that those who use the play will adhere to the general story and its ultimate message of hope and understanding.

Bobby H. Johnson

BLACKBOARD MESSAGE - A reproduction of a blackboard with its ironic message found in the ruins, as rendered by the Museum. (Photo courtesy of New London Museum)

NEW SCHOOL - A view of the building at New London. Construction began soon after the disaster. The building is still in use by the West Rusk School District. (Photo courtesy of the author)

OVERVIEW

A play in two acts with brief introductory and closing scenarios. It concerns the tragic natural gas explosion that destroyed the New London, Texas, junior-senior high school in March 1937. The accident resulted in the deaths of about 300 persons, mostly students in grades five through eleven. Such a devastating event brought untold human suffering to an emergent rural community in the burgeoning East Texas oil field. A bright spot in an otherwise depressed state and region during the 1930s, East Texas, and, New London in particular, represented the triumphs of modern technology over ancient agricultural existence. The school, built in the early part of the decade, played a central role in this transformation. It was touted as fire-proof and safe, heated by the natural gas that lay under the surface of the earth. Moreover, the school district was one of the wealthiest in the nation, enriched by the very energy that produced the disaster.

Each act is composed of several scenes featuring characters involved in the tragedy in a kind of "before and after" format. Act One begins with a school-community reunion set in 1987, the fiftieth anniversary of the disaster. Act Two concludes with a return to the reunion scene. In between, the play revolves around why such things happen and a series of "little stories" about people involved in the disaster. The major plot concerns the effects of the tragedy upon Harry Jones, a young oil field worker and father who, because of his job with an oil company, participated in the rescue (mainly recovery) effort. His struggles in the ensuing days (and years) portray the impact of tragedy on a human being who was unprepared for what he saw and felt. He is comforted by his wife, Bonnie, who draws upon her reservoir of faith and compassion. Her bravery in defending school officials accused of negligence surprises even her.

Minor plot lines involve several other characters, including a high school student and his younger brothers, one of whom dies in the explosion; a young female student who experiences the loss of her boyfriend; a teacher whose life was spared because he asked another teacher to cover his last period class that day, only to experience guilt because his friend died; a young woman who wandered from the explosion scene and later found a friend's body; and the school superintendent, who is overwhelmed by the disaster and the death of his own son. These characters will be treated in a series of scenes and soliloquies throughout Act One. Soliloquies will be delivered from a circle of light onstage. Other viewpoints will be expressed in several mock interview scenes scattered throughout Act Two; these are set up in the first reunion scene when an announcement reveals that an interviewer is present to take comments. They will be delivered from a chair at stage left. A character known as "Preacher" will be fundamental to the play's message. He will appear throughout as a kind of spokesman for the community, both in scenes and soliloquy.

The climactic explosion and ensuing turmoil (including a poignant "bucket brigade" and a fateful meeting between Harry and his wife) reveal the dramatic effect of the tragedy. The emotional high point of the play comes in the closing scene of Act One--the funeral of one of the young brothers. "Preacher" comments on the human frailty of death; he cites several Scriptures pertinent to children and tries to comfort the grieving parents. The setting, as in all scenes, will be minimal--perhaps a mound of dirt with a backdrop of gravestones. A small vocal ensemble (on stage) composed of several singers will present a few hymns, including the haunting "Sweet By and By" and "Rock of Ages."[1] Harry and Bonnie are present at the cemetery (Perhaps Bonnie is one of the singers.) A brief intermission (about 10-15 minutes) follows.

As lights come up on Act Two, "Preacher," still clad in his funeral suit, speaks from the Circle of Light. This is a poignant soliloquy in which he argues with God about why such things

1 These are suggestions. Directors may choose other songs as long as they were used in that era (1930s). Another choice is "No Tears In Heaven," a 1930's song of the "Stamps-Baxter" gospel variety, which was reportedly song at some of the funerals. This title is found as epitaphs on a few student graves at Pleasant Hill Cemetery.

happen. He refers to Psalms 55, verses l, 4, and 6--speaks of "the terrors of death" and longs for the wings of a dove so he can fly away and have rest. The scene ends with him on his knees, beseeching comfort and strength.

Another dramatic scene features Harry and Bonnie in a tense discussion on the back porch. Harry tries to express his anguish but becomes sick at his stomach. The thought of visiting his young friend in the hospital unnerves him, but Bonnie insists that he overcome his fear and carry out the visit. This ultimately leads to a hospital scene in which Harry tells his friend that God spared him for a reason. In the meantime, Bonnie serves food for grieving families gathered at a nearby church. It is there that she speaks out in defense of the school superintendent and school board, whom some parents hold responsible for the accident.

Other brief vignettes (as noted above) are interspersed among these scenes, with the intent of showing how the explosion affected several characters, some of whom were introduced in Act One. These may be survivors telling their stories, observers who witnessed the disaster, a man who worked in the rescue activities, a dramatic commentary by a mother who remembers her daughter who died in the explosion, a comment by the "young man," and a dispassionate commentary on the community by a long-time observer. These will be reflective, so characters should be dressed in more modern attire (late 1980s.) Those who first appeared in Act One will need to age.

A scene drawn from the findings of the military court of inquiry will offer a documented view of the causes of the explosion and proposals intended to deter similar events in the future.

The play ends with a dramatic return to the reunion where Harry is reunited with Henry, the young man now fifty years older. They recount their lives and Harry learns that his friend once gave a pint of blood to his (Harry's) son during a polio epidemic many years later. This completes the circle and leaves Harry and the "young man" with a sense of resolution concerning the explosion. In a brief epilogue from the Circle of Light, "Preacher" briefly reflects on what the future might bring--a reference or so to future disasters. As he speaks, actors solemnly enter for stage bows. The play concludes with a dramatic presentation of an old hymn.

HAROLD AND JOHNYE JOHNSON - Parents of the author. Their story is central to the play. (Photo courtesy of the author)

CHARACTERS

(Actors may play several roles with minor changes of costume and appearance.)

Harry Jones--A young (about 26 years old) oil field worker and father who becomes involved in the recovery scene. He is a happy man whose life is forever changed by what he witnessed. He loves children and baseball.

Bonnie Jones--A young (about 25) housewife. She is the mother of two sons, one a six-year-old first grader and the other an infant. She is a high school graduate who grew up in rural surroundings. She has a strong religious faith.

Gary Jones--Son of Harry and Bonnie. He is a first-grader who witnessed the actual explosion from a bus a mile or so away from the scene. His first appearance will be a mute stare out of a bus window.

Henry Willett--A seventeen-year-old high school student. He is seriously injured in the explosion. Friend of Harry. Reunited with Harry in the hospital and as adult at reunion; recounts his story in an interview.

George Willett--Middle brother of Henry--13 years old. He is killed in the explosion. His funeral is portrayed.

Tommy Willett--Younger brother (about 10) of Henry and George.

John Pilgrim --Young sweetheart--about 16. Best friend of Henry. Killed in explosion.

Mary Massey--About 16. Sweetheart of John. Later recounts her story after explosion.

Mrs. Smith--A first-grade teacher, about 28 years old. Discusses her plans for March 18 with husband. Later describes experience in Act Two.

Mr. Smith--High school science teacher--about 30 years old. He left the building shortly before the explosion.

Newspaper reporter--A then young woman, about 22 years old. As a mature woman in Act Two, she describes the heart-rending emotions she felt in covering the story.

Elizabeth Edwards--A sixth-grader who had a pen-pal in England.

Mrs. Edwards--Elizabeth's mother.

Singers--May play other roles with change of costume. (About five persons, two women, three men). They may play other roles and appear in reunion scenes as part of crowd.

Betty Rose--Seventeen-year-old high school student. She recounts her memories of the explosion.

Josh Slater--About 22 years old--works at recovery site as part of basket brigade. Recounts story in Act Two.

Jack Welch--Observed explosion from about a mile away. Tells of later religious experience in Act Two reprise.

"Preacher"--An older man--about 60 years old. He is a strong person shaped by his experience as a minister. He comes and goes throughout the play; serves as narrator and conducts George's funeral.

R.C. Hall--School superintendent, nearing retirement (about 58). A tall, thin man--on the verge of a nervous breakdown.

Major Pace--National Guard officer; president of Court of Inquiry.

Dr. John Abbott--University chemistry professor; expert witness at inquiry.

James Collins--*New York Journal* reporter. He covered the explosion story.

National Guard officers--Compose Board of Inquiry soon after explosion.

Johnnie McWilliams--Community old-timer.

Miss Nelson--Fifth grade teacher.

Four fifth grade children--2 girls, 2 boys

HORACE GRIGG - Injured in explosion. His experience is portrayed in the play. (Photo courtesy of Horace Grigg)

SCHOOL SUPERINTENDENT - W. C. Shaw, native East Texan and school administrator at time of disaster. His son, Sambo, died in the tragedy. Mr. Shaw died in 1962.
(Photo courtesy of New London Museum)

STAGE SETTING

The stage will be sparsely decorated. A Texas flag centered above the proscenium. Scenery and settings will be minimal. A back porch will be located stage left, consisting of a deck with steps and a shed roof supported by posts. A screen door will open into the house. It should be mounted so that it softly slaps when it is allowed to close. Rustic materials should be used. A number 2 washtub hangs on the wall, along with an outdoor thermometer in the shape of a soft drink bottle. The only furniture is a straight-backed wooden chair sitting to one side, with perhaps a few pot plants on a small bench. The representation is of a simple oilfield house.

Various scenes will be portrayed in the middle of the stage. Simple settings may be moved on and off as the various scenes unfold. These will include an auditorium setting with two rows of seats and a podium, a bench, a disaster mock-up with debris scattered around, a cemetery scene with an unearthed grave and a few funeral wreaths, a church kitchen with tables and chairs, a hospital room with bed and chair, and a hearing room with table and chairs. Darkness will prevail as settings are changed.

A raised platform will be located stage right, close to the front of the stage. This will be the circle of light for soliloquies.

An interview chair, stage left, near front of stage. Characters will relate their memories from this chair.

Lighting will be crucial throughout. Red and blue lights will be used to suggest mood changes. The circle of light (stage right) over the platform should flood the area to reveal the speakers, but it should be restricted to that area alone. A similar setting will focus on the interview chair (stage left). The speeches will suggest a somber but dramatic mood as the actors communicate directly with the audience or with the interviewer.

If desired, a slide presentation of East Texas and disaster scenes may be shown on a screen or flat surface to the side, perhaps at the end as cast sings final hymn. Appropriate music is heard over the sound system. Selections, drawn from the 1930s era, will suggest a Texas setting by featuring bands from that period with a strong guitar and fiddle presence. Hymns will be used to suggest the somber tone of the play.

ACT ONE

STAGE SETTING: *House lights fade as Preacher introduces play from circle of light. Reunion setting stage center. He reads from the book of Ecclesiastes (Chapters l and 3).*

Scene 1

The Circle Begins: *Tempus Fugit*

Lights up on podium.

PREACHER: From the book of Ecclesiastes: "What does man gain from all his labor and his toil here under the sun? Generations come and generations go, while the earth endures forever.

The sun rises and the sun goes down; back it returns to its place and rises there again. The wind blows south, the wind blows north, round and round it goes and returns full circle. . . .

For everything its season, and for every activity under heaven its time:

a time to be born and a time to die;

a time to plant and a time to uproot;

a time to kill and a time to heal;

a time to pull down and a time to build up;

a time to weep and a time to laugh;

a time for mourning and a time for dancing;

a time to scatter stones and a time to gather them. . . .

a time to embrace and a time to refrain from embracing;

a time to seek and a time to lose;

a time to keep and a time to throw away;

a time to tear and a time to mend;

a time for silence and a time for speech. . . ."

Lights down on podium.

Scene 2
Reunion 1987

Lights up on reunion scene center stage. Crowd is milling around, getting seated in chairs. People greeting each other, shaking hands, making small talk. Woman comes in with reluctant man following. They are dressed in 1980s clothing. He is wearing a shirt, tie, and suit; she is in a nice dress. Other attendees might be: Mr. and Mrs. Smith, Mrs. Edwards, Josh Slater, and additional people to make a reunion crowd.

HARRY JONES: I told you I didn't want to come, Bonnie. Why'd you drag me off to this reunion, all the way up here from Houston? I don't recognize anyone.

(*He looks around and nods to people seated in front of them. He fidgets as they settle into seats.*)

BONNIE JONES: Hush, Harry. This is the first time we've been back since we moved. I just wanted to see some of these people again. Oh, there's a lady I knew at church. (*She waves.*) She lived down the street from us when we were out there in the camp. She lost a son in the explosion.

HARRY: Well, I don't have very good memories of this place. You know how hard it was for me--digging those poor kids out of all that rubble. It still makes me sick to think about it.

BONNIE: Now, Harry, don't get all upset. I thought it would do you some good to come back. It's been fifty years since all that happened. You need to forget the bad things. The past is gone and we can't do anything about it. Think how hard it is for all these people to face those memories. We just need to accept the past and enjoy the present. (*As she speaks, the master of ceremonies comments on the day's events.*)

ANNOUNCER: (*Over P.A. system, which squawks as it comes on.*) Welcome to the fiftieth anniversary reunion of those who were touched by the terrible disaster on this site. We have a full morning planned, and we encourage you to participate as together we commemorate that event. For those who are interested in preserving the historical record, we have a trained interviewer who will be available in Room 24 to tape your memories. Now, will the audience please stand as we sing the school song.

(*A piano plays the first few chords and a male voice leads the group in "London, Oh London." Gathering sings:*)

> "London oh London your colors of blue
> Always remind us of loyalty true.
> Deep in our hearts are your standards of gold,
> May we ever laud you while ages roll."

(*As the song ends the crowd is seated and a middle-aged man, dressed in a suit, shirt and tie, begins to speak from the podium. Harry is somewhat disinterested in the proceedings.*)

SPEAKER: We are gathered here today to commemorate those who died on this date 50 years ago--March 18, 1937. . . . (*As speech begins, Harry fidgets and then begins to pay attention.*) But, in another sense, we are here to remember our own place in time and to encourage those who will come after us to do likewise. Memorials are more important to the living than to the dead because they keep us in touch with the past and point us toward the future. (*On "Memorials," the lights begin to fade and the stage goes dark.*)

Scene 3
Setting the Stage

Reunion set is removed. Introduction by Preacher. Lights up on podium. A tall man steps in and begins to speak. He is dressed in a 1930s style suit--shirt and wide tie. He is self-confident but humble. He speaks in a strong voice, as though he were in a pulpit preaching. A musical interlude. Scene shifts to back porch, stage left. This setting remains on stage throughout the play. Lights up to signify early morning. A young Harry emerges from back door, dressed in khaki work clothes. Screen door slaps. He carries work boots which he proceeds to put on while seated on porch steps. He whistles an anonymous tune as he laces boots and then stands to stretch. Radio plays music from inside back door: theme music from "Light Crust Doughboys," followed by a lively tune. Announcer comments on tune and band, and then gives a brief weather report.

PREACHER: My name is John Black, but most folks around here call me "Preacher." I've lived in East Texas all my life. My people came here from Alabama--run out by hard times after the Civil War. I'm a Baptist to the core, but I believe in the brotherhood of man. We all need to get right with the Lord--sooner or later--because you never know what tomorrow might bring. . . . When the people of this community woke up on March 18, 1937, they had no idea of what lay ahead. It was early spring--the grass was just waitin' to jump up and the trees were swellin' with buds. The day began a little cool, but by mid-afternoon it had warmed up a bit, with just a hint of rain in the sky. Out in the oil field, people were beginnin' to stir. They were early risers, these people; this was a working community.

(*Lights down to low level. Preacher remains on riser, sitting on a stool so he can watch.*)

RADIO ANNOUNCER: "There you have it folks, 'Listen to the Mocking Bird,' coming to you at 6:45 a.m., Thursday, March 18, 1937. The weather here in East Texas is normal--moderate today but look out for rain tonight. Now, here's another tune from . . . . (*Fades away as Bonnie turns radio down.*)

BONNIE: (*From inside house.*) Hurry up, Harry. Your breakfast is almost ready.

HARRY: I know--I can smell the bacon. Got any biscuits? I've got a big day ahead of me--gotta change charts on all those gas wells.

(*He ambles around back porch--checks thermometer, moves a bucket from one place to another. A young woman emerges from kitchen with coffee cup which she hands to husband. She is clad in a simple house dress.*)

BONNIE: Here's your coffee--it's that new Admiration brand. (*She pulls up a small stool and sits down.*) Harry, do you think we did the right thing? I mean, moving down here to East Texas? Sometimes I feel so lonesome. Oh, I know that Sis lives over there in Gladewater. She's a lot of company, but I miss Mama and Papa. Oklahoma's so far away. (*She stares off into space.*) I don't know many people here.

HARRY: (*Looks at wife.*) Sure you do. You've got all those friends over at the church. And you're a room mother for the first grade. This is a good place to live. We've got two healthy sons and a nice little house (*He looks at house admiringly.*) Built it myself. I work for the best outfit in the oil patch. I know people who'd give their right arm to work for the Company. They pay me well--it sure beats staring at that mule's rear up there in Oklahoma. Yep, I'd say we've got it pretty good, and once this depression's over, things might really take off.

BONNIE: (*She stands up and opens screen door.*) I need to get Gary up for school. Breakfast will be ready in a minute. The baby's still got a cold, so I don't guess I'll go anywhere today. I'll have to miss the PTA meeting. Gary's gonna stay after school and play with Jimmy, then Mrs. Brown will bring 'em home after the meeting's over. (*She enters house and calls out*) Get up Gary--school bus'll be here soon.

HARRY: I hope it don't rain. I promised those Willett boys I'd play catch with them after school's out this afternoon. Remind me to put my ball glove in the truck. (*He enters house. Lights down.*)

Scene 4

Circle of Light

Lights up on podium. Preacher continues.

PREACHER: When old Dad Joiner brought in this field back in 1930, he set off a real boom. People came here from all over the country. They were lookin' for jobs, and they weren't disappointed. East Texas turned out to be the largest oil field in the world. Yes, sir, it was something to behold! You could climb up on a derrick and look out on those wells scattered among the pine trees. It was really impressive--'specially at night with the flares burning. People lived all over the place--out on leases or just anywhere they could rent a little piece of land to put a shotgun house on. Of course, the bigger companies had their camps with nicer houses--paved streets, and even playgrounds for the kids. These camps were mainly for the bosses and office workers. The real workin' people lived in what they called the "poorboy camp." But those distinctions didn't make a lot of difference--people were people. We all took pride in the good schools of this area. Here at London we had one of the best schools in the country--good teachers, science labs, a band hall. Why, we even had a lighted football field.

Children could hardly wait to get to school that morning. Some walked if they lived nearby, but most of them rode the school bus. Those buses comin' down the lane were a welcome sight to the people of this district. Yes, sir, old Dad Joiner brought a lot of change to East Texas. (*Lights down to low level.)*

Preacher remains on riser, sitting on a stool so he can watch. As he ends monologue, stage hands have been placing the necessary props for a series of upcoming scenarios. These will move across different parts of the stage, with lights serving as the trigger for beginning and ending. As one scene ends, another begins. Props will be minimal: a bus stop, a kitchen, a dining table, and a bench on campus.

Scene 5
The Day Begins

Outdoor scene. Four boys are gathered at a bus stop. Two older boys--about 17 years old--stand talking, while a younger boy, about 13, lingers nearby, wanting to be included. He tries to talk, but older brother ignores him. Youngest boy, about 10, wanders around scene, running after a butterfly which he catches and then releases. He picks flowers from ground. They are all dressed for school and carry books.

HENRY WILLETT: (*Talking to friend John.*) Boy, I hope that teacher has a little mercy on me today. I didn't get to finish my homework in geometry. That stuff is hard--I don't know why we have to learn about triangles and hypotenuses. I want to study agriculture--I bet those bulls don't worry about stuff like that. (*Chuckles*) Did you get your problems done, John?

JOHN PILGRIM: Yeah, I finished up about ten o'clock. Geometry kinda fascinates me. Besides, I want to be an engineer, and you've got to learn those things. They'll never let me in Texas A&M if I don't know my math.

HENRY: Say, John, maybe we can be roommates over there at A&M when we get out of high school next year. You could help me with my math.

GEORGE WILLETT: (*He pushes between Henry and John.*) I want to go to Baylor--I'm gonna be a Baptist preacher! Mama says she wants one of her boys to make a preacher.

HENRY: (*He pushes George away.*) Oh, shut up, George. You'll probably never get out of the seventh grade.

GEORGE: (*George withdraws, looking hurt.*) You shouldn't say things like that, Henry. What if I get hurt or something?

(*Henry jumps at him, and George retreats.*)

HENRY: Get out of here! (*Continues conversation with John.*) John, what are you gonna do about Mary when you go to A&M. They don't let girls in over there. You can hardly wait to see her every day. I bet you'll be out there on that bench sweet-talking her as soon as we get to school this morning. (*He smiles as he hits John on the shoulder.*)

JOHN: Well, I guess I'll worry about that when I get to it. Besides, I'm not as girl-crazy as you think. (*He gives Henry a friendly push.*)

HENRY: Come on over to the house when we get home this afternoon. Mr. Jones is gonna come by and play catch with us.

TOMMY WILLETT: (*Excitedly.*) Bus is coming! Bus is coming! Let me on first.

(*Lights down as boys shuffle toward bus and exit.*)

Scene 6

The Eyes of a Child

Lights up on a kitchen scene: Mrs. Edwards stands at an ironing board; her 10-year-old daughter, Elizabeth, sits at kitchen table doing school work.

MRS. EDWARDS: You're mighty late with your homework, Elizabeth. School starts in about an hour. What are you working on?

ELIZABETH: I've got to write a letter, Mama. My class is trying to become pen-pals with a school over in England. Where is England, Mama?

MRS. EDWARDS: Oh, it's somewhere over there in the Old World. Your family came from there a long time ago. (*She adjusts garment on ironing board.*)

ELIZABETH: What should I say, Mama?

MRS. EDWARDS: Well, you could tell about where you live and about the school. (*She continues to iron.*)

ELIZABETH: (*Thinking, she holds pencil against her head.*) I'm ten years old and I live in New London, Texas. It's in the biggest oil field in the world. We have a nice school where we learn about ourselves and other people. Yesterday in geography class, we studied where we live and what people do. In the past people farmed, but now most of them work in the oil field. Oil and gas are very important in East Texas. . . . (*She begins to write.*) I'll have this finished in a minute. Would you mail it for me, Mama?

MRS. EDWARDS: Sure, Libby, but you've got to hurry. School takes up in a little while. Here, let me fix your hair while you write. (*Lights fade as Libby writes. . . . Mrs. Edwards puts a blue ribbon in her hair.*)

Scene 7

Teacher Talk

Lights up as scene changes to another house where a man and wife--both teachers--discuss the upcoming day. He is seated on a stool, reading a newspaper. She busies around making coffee, turns and hands him a cup.

MRS. SMITH: Here's your coffee, Tiny. You'd better put that paper down and get a move on. It's almost time for school.

MR. SMITH: (*He puts paper down and takes cup. She pulls up a chair and sits as they talk.*) What's on your schedule today?

MRS. SMITH: Oh, just school. We're doing "Dick and Jane" in the reading circle. I'm telling you, teaching those first graders to read is a real challenge. It's fun to see their little eyes light up when we sound out those new words. (*Pauses*) We've got the PTA program in the afternoon. I think they're moving it out to the gym instead of the auditorium. We need more room. My group's doing a folk dance. I'll be home in time to fix supper, but we'll miss you. I wish you didn't have to be gone tonight.

MR. SMITH: Well, I want to get down there and check on the home place, but I hope to be back for the track meet tomorrow afternoon. Buford said he'd cover my sixth period class so I can get an early start.

MRS. SMITH: (*She gets up and prepares to leave.*) Oh, me, it's time to go. Be careful. (*She kisses him on cheek as she picks up purse and leaves. Lights down.*)

Scene 8

Puppy Love

Lights up as boy and girl sit on a campus bench. Greenery in background. Bird calls will sound as they talk. It is obvious that they are sweet on each other--at times they hold hands and cast loving glances.

MARY MASSEY: (*She is wearing a plain school dress.*) I dreamed about you last night, John. It was scary--a storm came up and the wind blew hard. I kept trying to find you, but the trees had blown down and I couldn't get through them. You kept calling out. I felt so. . . helpless. (*She pauses before finishing the sentence. She reaches for his hand.*)

JOHN PILGRIM: (*Dismissively.*) I don't know--dreams never made much sense to me. Maybe it's gonna rain. I have a hard enough time with my geometry. I was still working problems at 10 o'clock last night.

MARY: Oh, you're always worried about school. (*She pouts.*) Do you think we could meet at the movie tomorrow night? There's a double feature at the Strand. I'll get my mother to run me over there after I get home from the county meet in

Henderson. We don't have school tomorrow; I don't think I could stand it I didn't get to see you. (*She looks at him fondly.*) I'll be real nice to you. . . .

JOHN: I don't know--I'll probably be working on my geometry. (*He grins. She poutfully hits him on the shoulder.*) I'll try to get there. . . . (*Pause*) Do you think maybe we're seeing too much of each other, Mary? I've got to keep up my school work so I can go to college.

MARY: Well, if you like your geometry more than you like me, maybe I can find someone else. (*She cuddles up to him.*) It's time for class. Mr. Smith will kill me if I'm late again. See you at lunch. (*She kisses him on the cheek and leaves.*)

JOHN: Yeah, sure, at lunch. (*He longingly watches her leave. End of scene--lights down.*)

Scene 9

School Business

School office setting. School superintendent, R.C. Hall, sits behind desk which holds a big stack of papers. He is sorting out his work day. Secretary, Miss Ball, sits at end of desk with steno book in hand.

R.C. HALL: We've got a busy day ahead of us, Miss Ball. I still haven't finished all these forms for the County Meet tomorrow. (*He flicks through papers.*) Remind me to meet Mr. Wright over at the cafeteria for lunch--board business. Then we've got the PTA meeting this afternoon--you know we moved it out to the gymnasium. (*He leans back in chair and reflects.*) I'm telling you this has been one hard year. Getting that new gas system installed was a big job. It was a lot simpler when we heated with wood. Retirement looks better every day, Miss Ball. But that won't get me through today. (*He looks at papers on desk.*) Well, I better get busy. (*Lights down.*)

Scene 10
Hall Talk

Lights up on two girls talking in hall. They are carrying books. One girl has a dress folded over her arm.

BETTY ROSE: (*She is wearing a white blouse and skirt.) (Self-confidently.*) I saw you out there talking to John, Mary Massey. I bet you didn't even eat lunch. You can't live off of love, you know.

MARY MASSEY: Oh, Betty! I just spent a little time with him. Besides, I won't get to see him again 'til tomorrow night. That typing contest seems to take all of my time. I'll be glad when it's over.

BETTY: You think you're busy! I've got to get this prom dress finished so I can get a grade in sewing lab this six weeks. My mother says she won't let me go to the prom if I don't make an "A." I don't have time for boys. Well, not until the prom, anyway. (*They both giggle.*) I hope I get a date.

MARY: Oh, you'll get a date, Betty, even if I have to arrange it. Someone will ask you. (*She looks off into space.*) It sure is nice to have a steady boy friend, though.

BETTY: Well, I can always hope. I'm off to sewing lab. See you, later! (*Lights down as they hurry off.*)

Scene 11
Explosion Montage

Lights up on podium.

PREACHER: (*He turns toward audience.*) Alexander Pope's "An Essay on Man" says "Hope springs eternal in the human breast." Back when I was a school boy in this very community, we used to memorize a lot of poetry. I remember another poet who said "Into each life some rain must fall." Longfellow, "The Rainy Day."... Sadly, a storm was about to descend on New London, Texas. I want to warn you that what follows is not for the weak of spirit. In fact, it's downright disheartening, because all those hopes and plans we just heard about were dashed "in a moment--in the twinkling of an eye" as the Scriptures say. (*He pauses to compose himself.*) The school blew up a little after 3 o'clock, only a few minutes before the school day ended. It came with a mighty roar. . . .

Loud sound over sound system; lights flicker. Light on platform fades slowly and a brief moment of darkness prevails before a series of vignettes portrays how people perceived the explosion. These will flow across the stage as red and blue lights play on a scrim in the background. The effect should be kaleidoscopic, somewhat like a silent movie.

Lights up on a schoolroom scene stage right. Several students are misbehaving--throwing erasers and chalk at each other. They are startled, and several fall on floor as if crushed down. Others slump in desks in a tableau as lights dim but do not go completely out. Action moves to a man sitting in an office. He jumps up with a startled look on his face and stares out a window. Lights dim. A girl working at a sewing machine is startled by noise; she slowly stands up and puts garment over her arm as lights dim. Harry Jones is working on a piece of equipment, with wrench in hand. He looks into distance and freezes. Bonnie Jones rushes onto back porch (screen door slaps) and furtively looks toward right. Young boy (about six years old) looks out the back window of a school bus (portrayed by a bus mock-up with letters under window proclaiming SCHOOL BUS STOP). He stares big-eyed toward audience. Lights fade across stage. Darkness pervades a few moments.

Scene 12
Aftermath

Circle of light on platform. "Preacher" makes a few comments as props are moved on-stage. These might consist of representations of wreckage--slabs of concrete, rubble, boards and beams awry. Smoke (actually dust) fills air. Calmer lights on scrim.

PREACHER: (*He speaks with difficulty--pauses between statements.*) It was a nightmare-come-true. The building just blew up--tiles and mortar went everywhere--great big slabs of concrete. And all those poor children! About three hundred died plus several teachers. It would have been a lot worse if the PTA meeting hadn't been moved to the gym behind the school. Relief workers showed up immediately--most of them were oil field hands. They cleared that scene over the next eighteen hours or so, using their oil field equipment--they strung up lights and worked all night. (*Pause*) Some of them even found their own children underneath all that wreckage. They set up a bucket brigade--used peach baskets to remove the rubble. (*Pauses*) I hope I never live to see another scene like that.

(*Disaster scene as set above. Men in work clothes are involved in various chores--some lifting objects or pulling on ropes. Some movement on stage as relief workers hurry across stage--running here and there.*)

FIRST RESCUER: Over here--I found something.

SECOND RESCUER: Watch out--grab that beam.
(*Controlled confusion prevails. Lights come up on a line of about six or so men handing off baskets down the line. They speak as they work--encouraging each other and sometimes emitting cries of despair.*)

RESCUER: "Oh, my God, this is terrible."

RESCUER: "Here, keep it moving."

(*This should be a slow motion scene.*)

HARRY JONES: (*Bending over, handing off basket. He comments to man next to him.*) I don't think I can go on--I'm sick at my stomach.

FELLOW WORKER: Hang on, pal. Take a deep breath. We've got to keep the line moving.

HARRY: (*He visibly sighs.*) I'm OK, but I've gotta take a break. (*He moves away from the line and wanders off away from light.*)

FELLOW WORKER: Here! Someone give us a hand--we need another man on the line.

(*Another worker steps in for Harry. Lights fade as line freezes. Harry ends up stage center in front. He sits on a piece of debris and wipes his face with handkerchief. He is visibly shaken. Lights up as Bonnie approaches and speaks.*)

BONNIE: Harry, is that you? (*She moves to Harry and embraces him.*)

HARRY: What are you doing here, Bonnie? It's dangerous.

BONNIE: I had to see you, Harry. Gary's OK--he caught the bus home. I left him and the baby with the neighbors.

HARRY: (*Interjects.*) How'd you get here?

BONNIE: I've been trying for an hour, but there's so much traffic on the road. I finally just walked. (*They stand with arms around each other as Bonnie looks on scene.*) It's horrible, Harry. I never expected to see anything like this. Are you OK?

HARRY: (*He stares off for a moment before replying.*) I don't know, Bonnie. This is the hardest thing I've ever had to do. (*Pause*) We found a couple of kids alive, but mostly it's been bodies. I've been sick at my stomach most of the time, but I had to go on. . . . I could have found my own son. (*He turns away.*)

BONNIE: But you didn't, Harry. I told you, Gary forgot to stay after school. He caught the bus and came home. He's OK. I brought you some sandwiches. (*She fumbles in a sack she carries.*)

HARRY: Thanks, but I can't eat anything. (*He looks away into space.*) You'd better go, Bonnie. I think they're trying to clear out this area. Hug the boys for me. I've got to get back on the line. We'll be here all night. (*He looks up--holds hand out and says*) "It's gonna rain." (*He moves away. She watches him leave. Lights down.*)

Scene 13
The Inquiry

Lights up on campus scene--spotlights in background, line of men. A scholarly man approaches a military officer in uniform and introduces himself. They converse about the need for an investigation.

DR. JOHN ABBOTT: Major Pace? I'm John Abbott. I just got in from Austin. The governor's office flew me over here to help with the investigation. (*He looks around.*) I had no idea it was this bad.

MAJ. PACE: Thank you for coming on such short notice, Doctor. (*They shake hands.*) As you know, the governor's office is very much involved in this situation. In fact, we've just been notified that the governor is declaring martial law so we can get a better hold on things here--there's too much confusion with all these people walking around. The Governor will want some kind of inquiry--that's where you come in. Most people don't know how dangerous gas can be. We're fortunate to have someone of your experience.

DR. ABBOTT: Thank you, Major. I've been trying to educate people about gas for the past twenty-five years. Petroleum is a wonderful thing, but you have to be careful with it. I'll need to do some field work in the morning--ground samples and that sort of thing. (*He looks around.*) A lot of the evidence is buried under all this rubble, but at the rate they're going (*He nods toward workers.*) We should be able to find what we need. (*Pauses*) This is terrible. (*Lights dim, but explosion scene remains under faint light.*)

Scene 14
Bad Dreams

CIRCLE OF LIGHT: A series of soliloquies by survivors: Mary Massey, R.C. Hall, Mr. Smith, and Betty Rose. This is a lead-in to the funeral.

MARY: (*She is disheveled--dress smudged, has cut on forehead, hair amiss. Carries books clasped to her chest.*) It was like a nightmare. . . . I was in study hall, waiting for the last bell to ring--I had my books in my arms--ready to go. I had just stood up when everything shook. A large piece of concrete smashed the table where I'd been sitting, and there was dust everywhere. I heard a boy call for me to jump out the window with him, but when I looked out and saw all that destruction, I just couldn't do it. I finally found my way to the stairwell. I kind of scrunched under the wreckage and got outside. I looked for John, but . . . I couldn't find him. (*She stares at audience as light dims. Steps from podium and exits.*)

R.C. HALL: (*He is coatless, tie undone, and generally scruffy; he is distraught, so his speech is somewhat disorganized.*) Have you seen my boy? I can't find my son. . . (*he pauses*) I was out here talking with one of the janitors--I'd been over to the elementary building--something happened. Everything just went dark--seems like I heard a loud noise. I rushed to the building, but I couldn't find the door. All those children--gone. You found my boy? Oh, Lord, why didn't you take me? (*Lights down. He exits.*)

MR. SMITH: (*He is a big man, clad in shirt and slacks. His manner is calm, but he is obviously distressed. Lights up.*) I hadn't been out of the building fifteen minutes when it blew up. My plans were to visit my folks down in the next county. Since school was out the next day, I thought I'd get an early start. So I got my friend Buford to take my last period class. He was a good friend (*grimaces and stops speaking for a moment to compose himself.*) I lived about 50 yards from the back of the school. I'd just gone into the house to get my bag when I heard a loud noise. I ran outside (*he stops speaking again*)--I couldn't believe what I saw. A huge cloud of dust covered the whole campus--debris was still falling--some of it landed in my yard. Once I got my breath, I ran up to the site where the school had been. It was just a pile of rubble. A good many people were just wandering around in a daze. I heard some screams. I finally worked my way around to where my room had been but it was buried under tons of wreckage. No one survived in that room. (*He stares vacantly; lights down.*)

BETTY ROSE: (*She is dressed as before but blouse is pulled out of skirt. She still carries a dress folded over her arm.*) I don't know how I got out. About twenty of us girls were in the sewing lab. I was working on my prom dress when it happened. There was a loud noise and then everything went black. When I came to I was standing in a crowd on the football field behind the school. I had my dress on my arm. I wasn't injured except for a few cuts on my face. I must have looked like a ghost because I was covered in a powdery dust from all the mortar and dirt in the air. Later, I remember finding the body of one of my friends --I led her mother to the spot where she lay. When I looked up, I saw my father about a hundred feet away. He was looking for me. (*Lights down on podium.*)

Scene 15

The Funeral

Cemetery setting, with backdrop of trees, gravestones. A mound of earth, covered with flowers. This might be a unit which can be placed on stage in darkness. It should be center-stage with other areas dark. A small crowd of mourners is visible standing around grave, with Preacher, Bible in hand, centrally featured. He stands on a soft drink case. Dressed in his Sunday best (suit, shirt, and tie), he will be the leading figure in this scene. A small chorus will sing a hymn or two, beginning as stage is being set in darkness. Hymn: "Rock of Ages." Lights come up slowly.

Rock of Ages

Rock of Ages, cleft for me.
Let me hide myself in thee;
Let the water and the blood,
From Thy wounded side which flowed,
Be of sin the double cure.
Save from wrath and make me pure.

While I draw this fleeting breath,
When my eyes shall close in death,
When I rise to worlds unknown,
And behold Thee on Thy throne,
Rock of Ages, cleft for me,
Let me hide myself in Thee.

(*As Harry and Bonnie enter cemetery, Mrs. Edwards is leaving cemetery. They speak in hushed tones.*)

BONNIE: I'm so sorry about Elizabeth.

(*Interaction between Harry and Bonnie and parents seated in a small row of chairs. The following hymn is sung as scene begins: darkness prevails.*)

Asleep in Jesus

Asleep in Jesus! blessed sleep,
From which none ever wakes to weep!
A calm and undisturbed repose,

Unbroken by the least of foes.
Asleep in Jesus O for me
May such a blissful refuge be!
Securely shall my ashes lie,
Waiting the summons from on high.

Sweet By and By

(*This hymn will be sung as sermon concludes, while Preacher comforts families.*)

There's a land that is fairer than day,
And by faith we can see it afar;
For the father waits over the way,
To prepare us a dwelling place there.

Refrain

In the sweet (in the sweet) by and by,
We shall meet on that beautiful shore;
In the sweet (in the sweet) by and by,
We shall meet on that beautiful shore.

We shall sing on that beautiful shore
The melodious songs of the blest;
And our spirits shall sorrow no more--
Not a sigh for the blessing of rest.

Refrain

In the sweet (in the sweet) by and by,
We shall meet on that beautiful shore;
In the sweet (in the sweet) by and by,
We shall meet on that beautiful shore.

Lights down--a gentle fade

PREACHER: Jesus said, "Suffer little children, and forbid them not to come unto me: for of such is the kingdom of heaven." We gather here to mourn the tragic death of such a child. George Willett did not have many days on this earth. He was only 13 years old. Little did he know what lay before him the day before yesterday. He went off to school, a happy seventh grader with the hope of a life-time before him. Now, he has gone to be with his Lord, along with hundreds of his school-mates, the victims of this horrible tragedy. The words I say today will have no effect upon George. He--and they--are safe. They rest in peace, asleep in Jesus. Rather, it is to you, his family and friends, that I direct my remarks.

This community needs to know that God cares in this time of tribulation. As the Psalmist said, "The Lord looketh from heaven. . . upon all the inhabitants of the earth." Today, the world cries for our community, even as we mourn the loss of these precious children. We do not understand why such tragedies happen--perhaps it is not for us to know. But we can be sure that the Lord knows and cares. As Job said long ago, God "discovereth deep things out of darkness, and bringeth out to light the shadow of death" (Job 12). We live in darkness and shadow, burdened by death and parting, but it shall not always be so. God has promised that if we cast our burdens on him, He will sustain us. Perhaps the poet said it best when he wrote: "God shall wipe away all tears; there's no death, no pain, nor fears; and they count not time by years, for there is no night there." We await that day. Lord, help us to believe. (*On the last line he looks up prayerfully. The scene ends as Preacher moves among the mourners, shaking hands and embracing them, while the chorus sings "Sweet By and By." Actors freeze as song ends. Lights fade and Act One ends.*)

INTERMISSION

ACT TWO

Scene 1

Circle of Light: Remonstrance

Stage is cleared of props except for Circle of Light podium and back porch. As scenes ensue, props are placed as needed. Interspersed between the scenes will be several reflective interludes as characters sit in a chair upstage left and talk to an invisible interviewer. Their comments are not necessarily tied to the scenes, but rather are intended to show human responses to the tragedy and to hint at the oral history process which underlies the entire play. Lights up on podium, where Preacher, still clad in funeral suit, begins a remonstrance with God. Interlude of guitar and fiddle music begins scene. Or perhaps a piano rendition of a few familiar hyms, which begins and ends with alma mater "London Oh London."

PREACHER: Lord, I need to talk to you. You know I've been a faithful servant ever since I promised to forsake the world and preach your word. I don't mean to grumble, but you're pushing me mighty hard, Lord. Oh, I know what you said about testing your followers. Why, I can even quote all the Scriptures--you know I can. But how do I explain to these people why they lost their children in this terrible disaster? I'm bending, Lord--don't let me break. As it says in your book, "My heart is sore pained within me; and the terrors of death are fallen upon me" (Ps. 55:4). I'm just a human being, Lord. If I had the wings of a dove, I could fly away and be at rest. But I don't have wings; all I have is these two arms, and right now I'm holding them up to you, Lord. (*He kneels at mention of "two arms."*) Like your servant David said long ago, "Hear my cry, O God; attend unto my prayer. From the end of the earth will I cry unto thee, when my heart is overwhelmed; lead me to the rock that is higher than I" (Ps. 66: 2-3). I'm waiting, Lord. Help me. Amen.

Lights down on podium.

REFLECTION I: J*ack Welch, an older man dressed in khaki pants and blue shirt. He speaks in a natural way, reminiscent of his East Texas background.*

That explosion was the worst thing I ever saw. I was about a mile away when it happened--over there in the company office doing some business. At first I thought a boiler had exploded somewhere out in the field, but when I looked out the window--I was on the second floor, you see--I had a good view of the school. It was just a cloud of dust. I ran down to my car and got over there in a few minutes. It was just utter confusion --people screaming, kids trying to get out of the rubble. I helped to put out a little fire where the science lab had been--that was the only fire I saw. I worked all that night, pulling out bodies and trying to comfort parents who just swarmed over the site. It reminded me of pictures I'd seen from World War I. You asked me if I was a religious man before all that happened. I regret to say that I was not. . . but I was soon thereafter!

Scene 2

After the Funeral

Lights up on oil field house. Harry Jones sits on porch steps with head in hands. He is visibly shaken. Wife Bonnie stands on porch with a plate of food in her hands. They are dressed in funeral clothes.

BONNIE: You've got to eat something, Harry. It won't do for you to get sick. (*She offers plate to him, but he rejects it.*)

HARRY: I can't eat, Bonnie. I'm sick to my stomach. I can't get it out of my mind--all those kids. Fifteen minutes and they would have been out of that building. Why do things like this happen? I don't understand it. Why?

(*Bonnie sets down plate. She wrings apron in her hands as she listens. She may sit on bench. Harry continues, voice distraught.*) That boy we dug out. He was so scared he was shaking, but he wasn't hurt bad. When we got all that stuff off of him, he got up and ran away. One of the fellows had to chase him down. He was lucky. (*He looks at Bonnie.*) That could have been our son. (*Pauses*) I saw one man uncover his own son's body. He just sat there and cried--holding that little body in his arms. We tried to comfort him, but he didn't want to let him go. The funeral home people finally took the body away, but the father just sat there and sobbed. I couldn't stand it. I had to leave.

(He looks at her and then suddenly runs out of sight. The sound of him retching pierces the scene. Bonnie jumps up and comes to steps, staring after her husband. He soon reappears, wiping his mouth with handkerchief.)

BONNIE: I know you saw some bad things, Harry, but you've got to get hold of yourself. (*He sits down on edge of porch, staring into space. She puts her hand on his shoulder.*) This thing that happened--it's horrible. I can't think of anything worse. But what's done is done. We just have to accept it and go on. I still think you need to go over to the hospital and visit Henry. He needs all the help he can get. (*She moves toward door.*) I've got to take some food over to the church--there's a lot of people to feed with all these relatives coming in. Mrs. Brown next door will look after the boys while I'm gone. I'll see you later. (*She hesitates.*) Gary wants to talk to you a little bit--he's upset by all of this. Be brave, Harry.

(*Harry stares after her as she goes into house. Gary meekly comes out door. Harry picks up Gary, hugs him, and then sets him on edge of porch next to him.*)

GARY: I saw the school blow up, Daddy. We were on the bus --I saw it out the window.

HARRY: I know you did, son. I'm glad you were on the bus. Your mother was worried. (*He looks away.*)

GARY: Why did it blow up, Daddy?

HARRY: I don't know why, son. It was just. . . an accident. Things like that happen.

GARY: Will we have school anymore?

HARRY: Sure, you will, Gary. After a while. . . when all of this has passed. You better hurry up now. Your mother's waiting. She's got to go up to the church and help some people. You take care of your little brother--OK? (*Harry hugs son and turns him toward the door. Gary pauses at door.*)

GARY: Will you come home tonight, Daddy?

HARRY: I'll be here, son. Don't worry. (*End of scene. Lights down.*)

REFLECTION II: *Oil worker Josh Slater offers his memories from interview chair. He confirms Harry's experiences and offers his own commentary on the tragedy.*

My name is Josh Slater. I was working in a roustabout gang out on a lease not far from the school--about three miles, I'd say. It was almost quitting time when we heard this loud boom and the ground just seemed to shake. A few minutes later a guy drove up and said, "you won't believe this, but the New London school just blew up." He'd been passing by and saw all the destruction--said it was terrible. We loaded up our tools and went straight up there. Our truck had a winch on it, so we got through the traffic and went right into the scene. It was mass confusion, but they finally got things organized. All the companies sent their crews. We lifted debris and helped get bodies out. I had a new pair of work boots; they were completely shredded by the time we got through the next morning. I worked in that bucket brigade--we actually used peach baskets. Hundreds of people worked all night--they finally let us go about 10 the next morning. There was a hard rain that night--but it didn't bother us. I don't remember being tired--we just kept working. The Salvation Army was there to provide food and coffee. I saw some terrible sights, but you just had to keep going. . . . It didn't hit me until the next day. I couldn't eat much--had a hard time sleeping for several weeks. It haunted me for years. I saw a lot of bad things during World War II, but nothing as bad as this. (*Lights down.*)

Scene 3

Throwing Stones

Lights up on church kitchen where Bonnie is serving family members. Several persons are milling around getting food. This may be portrayed in mime as they file by a table. Bonnie and another woman serve from behind table. They speak softly about the tragedy.

BONNIE: (*Speaking to friend.*) I feel so sorry for all of these people. Some of these families lost two children. (*Friend nods.*) How can they bear up under all this sorrow? Just think how bad the school board and Mr. Hall must feel. (*Friend nods again.*)

DISGRUNTLED FAMILY MEMBER: (*A tall, thin man overhears Bonnie's comment and reacts.*) That old man and the school board killed my kids. They should have known better than to change out the gas system. They've got blood on their hands. I say run 'em out. They're guilty. (*He breaks down.*)

BONNIE: (*She looks at man for a moment before speaking.*) I'm sorry you feel that way, Sir. Lord knows, we're all in shock. They didn't mean to hurt anyone. It was just an accident. Why, even Mr. Hall and some of the board members lost their own children. (*She moves to comfort him.*) I know it's hard on you and your family. I don't even know how I'd react if I lost a child. But we've all got to bear up and get through this. (*She helps him to a chair.*) Can I get you some water? (*Lights fade as she stands next to the man with her hand on his shoulder.*)

REFLECTION III: *Mrs. Edwards, whose daughter Elizabeth was killed in the explosion, comments on the loss of her child and* *the kindnesses of the community. She is about 80 years old.*

I lost my daughter Elizabeth in the explosion. She was 10 years old--in the fifth grade. (*She speaks slowly but firmly.*) I was able to identify her body by the dress she wore--it was blue, and it matched her eyes. Earlier that morning, I had fixed her hair and put a pretty ribbon in it. There's not a day passes --I'm nearly 80 years old--but what I don't think of her. It's a sweet memory.

Another thing I remember about that terrible experience is the kindness of my neighbors and friends. I don't know what I would have done without them. They fed us, kept the house clean, and took care of my other children. In the days that followed they supported me when the only thing I could do was sit around and cry. I'll never forget those wonderful people. . . (*Lights down--end of scene.*)

Scene 4

A Reason to Live

Lights up on hospital room setting--a bed, table, and chair. A young man, swathed in bandages, lies in bed. A nurse is tending him as scene opens. She exits and Harry enters, ball glove under arm and holding a sack of candy. He hesitantly speaks to Henry Willett, the patient.

HARRY: Henry? (*Henry is looking away but turns head and sees Harry.*) It's Harry Jones. I thought I'd come by and see how you're doing. (*Harry is visibly nervous. He takes off his hat and fiddles with it. He places bag on table.*) I brought you some candy. How're you feeling?

HENRY: Not too good, Mr. Jones, but I'm sure glad you came. I got a busted leg and a broken arm, but I'll be OK. It gets pretty lonesome up here. My folks had to go to the funeral--I guess they'll be back soon. I didn't get to go, and I'm really sorry about that. (*He turns head away. An awkward silence follows.*)

HARRY: I brought my ball glove--I don't know why. I guess I thought it might make you feel better just thinking about playing a little catch. We'll have plenty of time for that when you get out of here.

HENRY: Yeah, but George won't be there. (*He pauses and turns head away.*) I don't know if I can stand it, Mr. Jones. George and I were pretty good buddies, even though I was mean to him at the bus stop the other morning. (*Pauses*) I guess he won't get out of the seventh grade after all. (*He cries.*)

HARRY: George ain't hurting, Henry. He's gone to a better place. I'm just glad you're here. You'll get over this--shoot, a broken arm ain't too bad. At least it's not your throwin' arm. (*He pauses.*) I just want to tell you one thing, Henry. The Lord wasn't ready for you. There's a reason why you lived. You may not know why now, but one of these days you'll understand.

HENRY: (*He turns head toward Harry.*) Do you really think so?

HARRY: Sure I do. It may take a while, but you'll see. In the meantime, we've got a lot of ball to play. That young brother of yours--Tommy--he's got a lot of potential. I think he might make a pitcher. (*Lights fade.*)

REFLECTION IV: *Betty Rose, survivor, tells of how the explosion affected her life.*

I went to a lot of funerals after the explosion, including my own cousin's. It was a terrible time--unreal. It took me a good while to work through all that. Several of us went to Kilgore College the next year, and it was hard to sit through classes. Sometimes, you just had to go outside and gather yourself. The teachers understood, though, because they knew what we'd gone through. For a long time, I couldn't sit through a movie in the dark. In fact, it took me twenty-five years before I could talk much about the explosion. I didn't even tell my own children--I didn't want to scare them. We did visit some of our classmates in the hospital, and we even had our prom that spring. I wore the dress that I was working on when the school blew up. (*Lights down.*)

Scene 5

Bearing Up

Lights up on back porch. Bonnie comes outside (door slaps) and sits on bench. She is thinking when Harry walks up.

BONNIE: Hey, Harry. Where have you been? I was getting a little worried.

HARRY: I went over to the hospital to see Henry. (*He sits on steps.*)

BONNIE: How's he doing? Is he okay?

HARRY: Well, he's pretty banged up. Got a broken arm and leg, a bunch of cuts. But I guess he's pretty good considering what he went through. He's pretty low about his brother. I tried to cheer him up--told him there was a reason why he's alive.

BONNIE: (*She moves to steps beside him.*) Why, Harry. That was sweet. It makes you sound a little religious.

HARRY: I don't know, Bonnie. I've got a lot of things to work out in my head. How'd it go for you over at the church?

BONNIE: Oh, we had a lot of people come through. I felt kind of helpless--all of those poor people hurting so bad. I stood up for Mr. Hall and the other school people. I can see why some people might want to blame them, but . . . (*she looks into space*) what's done is done. We can't do anything about that. (*She rises and turns toward door.*) I need to feed the boys.

HARRY: I think I'll take a walk. I got a lot of thinking to do. (*Lights down.*)

REFLECTION V: *Lights up on interview chair. Mrs. Smith, the teacher, tells of her husband's guilt over his friend's death in the explosion.*

I was out in the gym at the PTA meeting when the school blew up. My group was doing a Mexican hat dance. Suddenly I heard this loud noise and it got really dark. After I got my students back to the elementary building, I worked my way over to our house--we lived just behind the school. My husband had been out of the building only a few minutes when it blew up. (*Pause*) He had an awful time dealing with that explosion. He felt guilty because he'd asked his friend Buford to cover his class that afternoon. He couldn't understand why he was saved and Buford was killed. . . . I guess a lot of people had the same question. (*Lights down on interview chair.*)

Scene 6

The Truth Shall Set You Free

Lights up on church steps. Harry reluctantly approaches steps. As he hesitates, Preacher comes down steps. After greeting each other, they talk about the disaster.

PREACHER: 'Evening, Harry. How's your family?

HARRY: They're fine, Preacher. At least, they're alive. I've been real busy, helping out with all this explosion stuff. . .(*He looks away.*) Preacher, there's something I need to talk to you about.

PREACHER: What is it, Harry?

HARRY: What you said at that Willett boy's funeral--you know, about having faith? Preacher, I find it mighty hard to have any faith in a God that let all this happen. I want to believe, but this is tearing me all to pieces.

PREACHER: It's a real problem, Harry. We all have doubts-

-that's natural. Tennyson once said, "There lives more faith in honest doubt, . . . than in half the creeds." You know how I like to quote poetry. Someone else said faith without doubt is dead faith. But I also know what the Scriptures say: "Faith is the substance of things hoped for, the evidence of things not seen." Keep hoping, Harry. God's big enough to handle your doubts. He didn't cause this disaster. It's his world, Harry, and death is just as much a part of life as being born. Sometimes we just have to hang on.

HARRY: Do you think I'll ever understand it, Preacher?

PREACHER: Some day, you will. You've just got to keep trying. (*Lights down.*)

REFLECTION VI: *Lights up on chair. Newspaper reporter describes her feelings while covering the explosion. She is in her early 70's.*

REPORTER: I was a 22-year-old reporter in my first job-- fresh out of journalism school at the University of Texas. I tell you, it was an awful scene. I lived in Nacogdoches, and I got a ride up there with an embalmer. We stopped at a funeral home in Henderson, where there was just a sea of parents waiting to go in and identify their children. We went right into a preparation room. When I saw those little bodies it just made me sick. (*Pause*) I caught another ride over to the explosion site--got there about 8:30 in the evening. It was like a movie set--they had lights and heavy equipment. I saw a lot of men picking at the rubble with their hands. I rode home in an ambulance; instead we had the body of a teacher from Nacogdoches. When I went back to the site the next morning, I happened to run into Dr. Abbott, a chemistry professor I'd known at the University of Texas. He was there as an expert investigator for the board of inquiry. (*Lights down on interview chair.*)

Scene 7
The Inquest

Lights up center stage on table with several chairs for military officers who are holding a board of inquiry. Dr. Abbott stands to one side as scene begins. He addresses audience as three officers seat themselves. After opening speech, he moves over behind table and sits to one side. This is a representation of the inquiry into the explosion. Witnesses will be heard but not seen. An empty chair is in front of the table. After several questions and responses, Dr. Abbott will move downstage to comment on the findings. and speak with a reporter.

DR. ABBOTT: (*He is clad in a suit, shirt, vest and tie. Officers wear khaki uniforms with ties.*) I was holding a seminar with my graduate chemistry students when the governor's message arrived. He asked me to assist in an investigation at New London. My preliminary inspection indicated that natural gas was involved, but I must confess that I first thought the explosion was due to gas that had somehow escaped into the hollow tiles of the building's walls. That was incorrect, and we later learned that a massive amount of gas had gathered under the foundation. This was based on the testimony of several persons who appeared before the court of inquiry. (*He moves to a chair behind the table. Lights up.*)

MAJ. PACE: This board of inquiry is convened to discover, as best we can, the cause of this disaster. Captain, would you begin the questioning?

FIRST OFFICER: (*He speaks as though a witness is seated before him.*) Sir, I believe you were one of the architects on the building. Tell us, please, about the heating system.

FIRST VOICE: (*Architect is heard from off-stage.*) The original plans called for a steam system with a remote boiler. That meant no gas lines under the foundation. The board later changed to a gas-steam system with individual gas-fed radiators throughout the building. We opposed such changes because of the potential danger but were unable to prevail. . . . (*Lights flick and come up again.*)

SECOND OFFICER: The school district later discontinued commercial gas service and tapped into a waste gas line. Did you, sir, as superintendent for the district, have any role in that decision?

SECOND VOICE: (*R. C. Hall off-stage.*) Yes, I was partly responsible for giving the order to change the gas supply. We thought it was safe because others in the community were already using it--it was going to waste. We used our staff--janitors and bus-drivers--to hook it up. . . . (*Lights flick.*)

DR. ABBOTT: Tell me, sir, as a member of the board of trustees, did you have any reservations about this situation?

THIRD VOICE: (*Board member off-stage.*) We had no knowledge that the use of waste-gas would be dangerous. The fact that others were successfully using it--including several churches--led us to believe it was safe. We did know that we could save some money. . . . (*Lights flick.*)

MAJ. PACE: I would like to thank the witnesses for appearing before this board. Our report will be forthcoming. This meeting is now adjourned. (*Lights down on table. Dr. Abbott moves downstage to conclude scene.*)

DR. ABBOTT: The Board found that the probable cause of the explosion was an explosive mixture of gas and air beneath the foundation of the building. It was likely set off by a spark from an electrical switch in the manual training room. (*Pause*) This disaster was largely due to ignorance of the dangers of natural gas and the absence of an odorizing element, plus other factors related to proper installation and maintenance. We must learn from this horrible experience. (*Lights down on table, other members freeze, Abbott picks up briefcase and walks to* *center stage front. He is stopped by a reporter, as he exits. Table removed.*)

Purpose of scene: to show journalistic presence--from New York. Reporter--James Collins--is a middle-aged man. He wears raincoat over sports jacket, perhaps unbuttoned. Also wears hat. Has notebook in hand. Speaks with northern accent--is somewhat brusque.

JAMES COLLINS: (*He approaches as Dr. Abbott finished his comment.*) Excuse me, Doctor, I'm James Collins with the *New York Journal*. Could I ask you a few questions?

DR. ABBOTT: (*He holds a brief case in one hand. Shakes hands with reporter.*) Of course, Mr. Collins.

COLLINS: I understand you're the expert on natural gas.

DR. ABBOTT: Well, I've had a little experience. What do you want to know?

COLLINS: It looks like to me these people messed up. Didn't they know this stuff was dangerous?

DR. ABBOTT: Of course, they know it's dangerous. These people live in the world's largest oil field. Maybe they became a little slack in handling gas because they live so close to it.

COLLINS: But it took the lives of several hundred children, Doctor. Why doesn't the state do something to make natural gas safer?

DR. ABBOTT: I think it will, Mr. Collins, I think it will. (*Lights down.*)

REFLECTION VII: *Lights up as older man speaks from chair*

OIL FIELD HAND: I don't care what that report said. I know what happened to cause that explosion. I worked not far from the school--switching tanks for a little oil company. In fact, I was in the building the night before it blew up--visiting with the night watchman. I helped him light some of the heaters; we didn't notice anything wrong. But a few days after the explosion one of the high school boys told me that they'd been jumping on a pipe that had been stubbed out in the hall--where a heater had been removed. They'd been doing that for a couple of weeks, but the morning of the explosion one of them stepped on it and he said it didn't spring back up. That tells me that it was broke. And that's where all that gas came from. Now don't that make sense? (*Lights down on chair.*)

Scene 8
Soul Searching

Back porch--About 8 a.m. Sunday. Harry is seated on steps reading a newspaper. Radio on in kitchen--gospel music. Announcer breaks in with funeral announcements. Bonnie comes out and they converse. She is clad in her Sunday dress.

BONNIE: Did you keep your breakfast down, Harry?

HARRY: (*He wears work clothes.*) Nope. My stomach's still upset. *(He leafs through paper.*)

BONNIE: Anything in the paper?

HARRY: Yep. A lot of bad news. Here's a list of those killed. (*Pauses*) Listen to this: It says that five members of the paper's circulation department were killed in the explosion. . . . (*He looks up.*) I guess that's why our paper wasn't here this morning. I had to walk up to the station to get one. (*He shuffles paper.*) Here's a story on the inquiry board--says Mr. Hall broke down while he was testifying, couldn't go on.

BONNIE: Poor man. I don't see how he got up there at all. Why do they have to do this so soon? People need time to heal. (*She walks over to Harry.*) Why don't you go to church with us this morning, Harry? It would do you some good.

HARRY: Can't do it. I've got to report to the shop. They told us to show up in case someone needs help. A lot of family members are still coming in. I'll probably have to help them find their folks out in the field. Don't wait supper on me--(*sighs*)--I probably won't be hungry anyway. (*Lights down.*)

REFLECTION VIII: *Lights up on chair. Tall man in western style jacket. He wears a western hat during interview.*

HENRY WILLETT: Yeah, I heard about that pipe. In fact, I even jumped on it. But I don't think that's what caused the explosion. If it had, it would have come out in the investigation. The legislature and the federal Bureau of Mines concurred with the inquiry board's findings. We'll never know what really caused it. . . . What did I do later? Well, after I got out of the hospital I started living again--graduated from high school the next year and went to work in the oil field. I thought about going to college, but after my friend John was killed, those dreams kind of went away. I got married, eventually had a family, and worked for the Company until I retired. That's when the best part of my life began. I bought a ranch in West Texas and grew sheep. We lived at the end of the road. Those sheep don't talk back. . . . Nah, I don't think much about the explosion. Sure, I missed my brother growing up. But you've got to keep going. (*Lights down on chair.*)

Scene 9

Shop Talk

Lights up on a small group of men in a shop setting. One sits on a keg, another sits on a chair turned backwards. Others are standing or squatting on floor. Some have coffee cups in hand. They converse about the explosion and its impact on them.

FIRST WORKER: Man, I've never been so tired in my life. I know it's been only a couple of days since all this started, but it seems like I've been up for two weeks.

SECOND WORKER: I know what you mean. After we got through there at the site--when was it? Friday morning?--I tried to get a little rest. But I couldn't sleep. Every time I dropped off, I woke up--kept thinking about all those kids. It's like a nightmare. I spent all day yesterday out at the cemetery digging graves. I guess that's where I'll be today.

THIRD WORKER: I don't even work here, but I got drafted over at Gladewater. The boss sent a bunch of us over to help out. I served as a pallbearer yesterday. They didn't have enough hearses to go around, so a bunch of the guys had to use their pickups to haul the coffins. I'm telling you, I hope I never see anything like that again!

FOURTH WORKER: Well, one thing you can say about this disaster--it's put East Texas on the map. I understand there's reporters in here from as far away as New York City. (*Harry Jones enters shop and squats down on floor. Other men speak to him; he acknowledges others by nodding. Worker addresses Harry.*) There's some do-nuts over here, Harry.

HARRY: Oh, I don't think I want any. I'm having a little trouble with my stomach.

SECOND WORKER: I understand you've been driving around the oil field.

HARRY: Yeah, that's what happens when you drive a company car and know where all the leases are. I took off a little while to attend that Willett boy's funeral. . . . (*Pause*) This has been the worst thing in my life, but I don't guess I need to tell you guys about that.

FIRST WORKER: I don't think we'll ever be able to forget it.

FOURTH WORKER: Well, not today. Here comes the boss.

(*Supervisor enters room--he wears shirt, tie and hat. A few workers stand up.*)

SUPERVISOR: I appreciate all you men coming in today. It's been a rough time for all of us, but we've still got things to do. I want you two guys (*nods to workers*) to get out to the cemetery. The rest of you can help out at the funerals. Jones, I need you to do some more driving. In fact, there's a guy waiting down by the gate right now. Take him out to the Shepherd lease and then report back to me. You'll all get time off when this is over. (*Lights down as men move to different parts of stage.*)

Scene 10

Out of the Mouths of Babes

Purpose of scene: to show how children reacted to disaster. Setting: a temporary class-room, about two weeks after explosion. Fifth grade students talk with Miss Nelson, their teacher. They sit in chairs--she stands. This is a representative scene, with about four students. Preacher introduces the scene.

PREACHER: (*From his circle of light.*) After things settled down a bit, the community began to function again. People got up and went back to work. School took up less than two weeks later. They had to scramble to find temporary rooms for what remained of grades five through eleven, but they finished out the term as best they could. Children are adaptable--they have to be--and they often see things in a different light than adults do. I guess that's what the Psalmist meant when he said, "Out of the mouths of babes. . ."

(*Lights down on podium and then go up on a temporary classroom where a teacher and several students talk about the explosion.*)

TEACHER: Children, this is a sad time for our community. I know some of you have lost brothers and sisters, (*pause*) and even some of you were injured in the explosion. (*One child has bandages and another an arm sling.*) It's a hard time for all of us, but school must go on. We'll be here in this temporary room until the term ends. You'll all need to cooperate as we try to get through this hard time. Perhaps some of you would like to talk about what happened. (*Three students speak of their experiences or feelings, but one is unable to talk.*)

FIRST GIRL: I lost my sister. She was 15 years old. I really miss her. Sometimes I go into her room and just look at her bed and her things. But she's not there. The preacher said she's better off, but I'm not sure I understand that. I might some day, but I wish I had my sister back.

FIRST BOY: My daddy had to work over there, Miss Nelson. He stayed all night, digging out all those children. When he got home the next day and we sat down at the table for lunch, he couldn't eat. He couldn't sleep, either. It's been more than a week since the explosion, and he still can't eat or sleep. I don't know what we're gonna do, Miss Nelson.

SECOND BOY: (*He looks at teacher and tries to talk, but nothing happens except for a few stutters and false starts.*) "I just. . . my friends are. . . I can't talk ma'am.. (*He stares into space as teacher touches his shoulder and reassures him.*)

SECOND GIRL: I don't want to talk. I just want to forget all of this. I don't know if I'll ever be able to talk--it's like a bad dream. You don't want to remember it, do you? (*Lights down.*)

REFLECTION IX: *Lights up on interview chair as an older man speaks. about community. Reunion set is placed on stage center.*

JOHNNIE MCWILLIAMS: People didn't talk much about the explosion. I came here about a year later--set up a little store across from the school. Been here ever since. It's a good community. People get along. I don't know--maybe that tragedy made them more aware of each other's feelings. It was hard on that generation of parents, though, losing all those children. I remember one fellow who lost both of his kids. His wife ended up in the insane asylum. I couldn't tell that it affected the kids that survived--and I got to know most of them. They just seemed to accept it better. After the school was rebuilt and the monument put up, the community just went on. Years later, we incorporated the town--I served several terms as mayor. Then we started having these reunions and people felt a little more comfortable about the past. Yes, Sir, I guess we're all survivors. (*Lights down on interview chair.*)

Scene 11
Making Plans

Lights up on reunion planning session. Table stacked with papers, scrapbooks, annuals. One middle-aged woman stands at table; older woman, middle-aged man, and a high school boy sit. This is a lead-in to the second reunion scene.

OLDER WOMAN: Well, here we are again trying to get this reunion organized. We've got a lot of envelopes to stuff. (*She handles a stack of papers.*) What are you looking at, Margie?

MARGIE: These old yearbooks are fascinating. (*She is leafing through a school annual.*) Here's a picture of one of my teachers. Oh, there I am--and my classmates--boy, have they ever changed!

MAN: Let me see. Yep, that's you--girl, have you ever changed. (*She frowns at him.*) You've gained a little weight since 1947. (*He picks up scrapbook.*) I like these scrapbooks. It's just like you borrowed someone's memories. (*He leafs through scrapbook.*) Here's a letter from a class of students somewhere. "Enclosed you will find two dollars and twenty-three cents which our class has donated. Please use it on the memorial marker." It's from--hey, that was a colored school on the other side of the county. Schools were still segregated then.

OLDER WOMAN: If you two don't get busy we'll never get out of here. (*She turns to high school student.*) Brian, I want you to take these fliers to school tomorrow and get the principal to pass them out. We'll need all the help we can get. Do you think some of the students will volunteer for cafeteria duty the day of the reunion?

STUDENT: Yes, ma'am. I've already got some lined up. They think it's neat to help out. Most of us don't know much about the explosion. I've lived here all of my life, but I never heard people say much about it.

OLDER WOMAN: Well, they have a hard time talking about it, Brian. A lot of them wouldn't even come when we first started having these reunions. It was just too painful. But I'm expecting a big crowd this time. . . if we can ever get it organized. (*She looks at man and woman who are still absorbed in the annuals. Lights down.*)

Scene 12

Boys Will Be Boys

Dark stage as John and George begin to speak from cemetery. Setting is a backdrop of trees, tombstones: a peaceful place. John opens scene by greeting George.

JOHN: Hey, George, you still got your ball glove? I thought we might play a little catch.

GEORGE: Yeah, it's around here somewhere. Let me look. Here it is. (*Lights up on two boys standing a few feet apart ball gloves in hand. John mimes a toss to George who returns it. They are wearing school clothes.*)

JOHN: Remember that morning we were waiting for the bus? Your brother promised me a game of catch after school, but we never got around to it.

GEORGE: Yeah, I remember. I was looking forward to it, too --until everything just went black. (*They continue to toss the ball in mime.*)

JOHN: Well, it's not so bad here--we've got all these nice trees and the sky. . . (*He looks up and pauses.*) My folks came by the other day. (*Pause*) They look a lot older.

GEORGE: I know. The world gets older, but I'm stuck at age 13. I never had the chance to grow up. My brother was right: I never got out of the seventh grade.

JOHN: Don't feel so bad, George. You could have become a Baptist preacher and not had any fun. (*Pause*) Come to think of it, I could have become an aggie. (*Pause*) Well, at least we don't have to worry about homework anymore or girl friends. I wonder what ever happened to Mary. She's quit coming out here like she did at first. Maybe it was puppy love.

GEORGE: But you're gone, John. You don't expect her to love a ghost, do you? (*Lights fade as boys continue to play catch.*)

Scene 13

Reunion Redux

Lights up on reunion set. Participants rise as session ends. People begin to talk, greeting others.

ANNOUNCER: This concludes the formal part of our reunion, but we hope you'll all continue to visit. Remember, lunch will be served in the cafeteria at noon. Thank you for coming.

BONNIE: (*She and Harry are dressed as in first reunion scene.*) See, Harry, it wasn't so bad. (*She looks around.*) I want to visit with some of these people. Why don't you mingle around for a while. You might see someone you used to know. I'll meet you in the cafeteria. (*She wanders off.*)

(*Harry looks around, hat in hand. Wanders upstage center. A tall man in a western hat calls to him. Harry turns to face him.*)

HENRY WILLETT: Harry, Harry Jones! Is that you? (*He approaches and shakes hands with Harry.*) It's been forty years since I saw you. Are you still playing baseball?

HARRY: Henry Willett! (*They amble toward a bench and sit down.*) I didn't expect to see you. Last I heard, you'd wandered somewhere out west.

HENRY: Well, I came back. You can't stay away forever. (*Pauses*) I never thought I'd be sitting here not fifty yards from where I almost died. (*He looks around.*) Time changes things, don't it?

HARRY: It sure does. I spent the most miserable night of my life right out there. (*Pauses*) Remember when I visited you over there in the hospital?

HENRY: How could I forget! You told me to hang on--that there was a reason why I survived. Well, I'm still hanging on. How's your boy?

HARRY: Which one?

HENRY: The one that had polio.

HARRY: How'd you know about that?

HENRY: I was working down there not far from Houston. We heard about your boy. When they said he needed blood, me and some of the guys at the plant came down there and donated, but I didn't get to see you. I was transferred to West Texas soon after that, so I kind of lost touch. I knew he'd survive because he had a pint of my blood, and I'm a survivor. You told me I'd understand why some day.

HARRY: (*He speaks slowly with some difficulty.*) That boy is fine, Henry. He'll turn 52 years old this fall. (*He looks toward audience.*) Now I understand. (*Lights fade.*)

Scene 14

Fading Shadows

Preacher steps into the circle of light. He is clad in his dark suit.

PREACHER: From the book of Ecclesiastes: "For who can know what is good for a man in this life... Who can tell. . . what is to happen next under the sun?" What happened to this community is beyond our understanding. Children dying before their time . . . mothers and fathers left to ponder why . . . a community knocked to its knees . . . while the world watches in disbelief. Like the Good Book says, it's hard to know what good can come of this. (*Cast members begin to enter in groups, their shadows cast on scrim.*) But we live in a world we didn't make, and it's sure that we're not going to get out of it alive. As the Scripture says, "it is appointed unto men once to die, ..." The Psalmist said we pass like fading shadows. But where do shadows go? Perhaps they reappear in some distant place, like the echoes that linger long after the voice is stilled. Now, I'm no great theologian, but I am a man of faith, and as sure as I'm standing here I believe that those shadows come back to life in a better place. (*As he finishes, lights come up on the cast as they sing "In the Morning of Joy."*)

> "When the trumpet shall sound, And the dead shall arise,
> And the splendors immortal Shall envelope the skies,
> When the angel of death Shall no longer destroy,
> And the dead shall awaken In the morning of Joy."
> Chorus: In the morning of joy, in the morning of joy,
> We'll be gathered to glory In the morning of joy;In
> the morning of joy, in the morning of joy,
> We'll be gathered to glory in the morning of joy."

As hymn ends, a small group of students freeze while walking towards center stage. Lights fade.

The End

CEMETERY TODAY - Note that a modern building has replaced the wooden structure used for funerals in 1937.
(Photo courtesy of the author)

MONUMENT - Happy students portrayed on top of monument erected soon after the disaster. Designed by Texas artist Herring Coe.
(Photo courtesy of the author)